WORLD OF VOCABULARY

AQUA

Sidney J. Rauch

Zacharie J. Clements

Assisted by Barry Schoenholz

Globe
Fearon

Photo Credits

World of Vocabulary, Aqua Level, Third Edition

Sidney J. Rauch • **Zacharie J. Clements**

ISBN 0-8359-1287-6

Printed in the United States of America

9 10 11 12 13   06 05 04 03

1-800-321-3106
www.pearsonlearning.com

AUTHORS

Sidney J. Rauch is Professor Emeritus of Reading and Education at Hofstra University in Hempstead, New York. He has been a visiting professor at numerous universities (University of Vermont; Appalachian State University, North Carolina; Queens College, New York; The State University at Albany, New York) and is active as an author, consultant, and evaluator. His publications include three textbooks, thirty workbooks, and over 80 professional articles. His *World of Vocabulary* series has sold over two and one-half million copies.

Dr. Rauch has served as consultant and/or evaluator for over thirty school districts in New York, Connecticut, Florida, North Carolina, South Carolina, and the U.S. Virgin Islands. His awards include "Reading Educator of the Year" from the New York State Reading Association (1985); "Outstanding Educator Award" presented by the Colby College Alumni Association (1990); and the College Reading Association Award for "Outstanding Contributions to the Field of Reading" (1991). The *Journal of Reading Education* selected Dr. Rauch's article, "The Balancing Effect Continue: Whole Language Faces Reality" for its "Outstanding Article Award," 1993-1994.

Two of the *Barnaby Brown* books, The Visitor from Outer Space, and *The Return of B.B.* were selected as "Children's Choices" winners for 1991 in a poll conducted by the New York State Reading Association.

Zacharie J. Clements is president of Inner Management, Inc. and one of the most sought after speakers in North America. He was formerly Professor of Education at the University of Vermont. He has taught in public schools from grade 6 through high school. Dr. Clements has developed and implemented training programs in the teaching of corrective reading and reading in secondary school content areas. He has conducted numerous teacher training institutes for the local, state, and national governments and has served as a consultant and lecturer to school districts throughout the United States and Canada. Dr. Clements has authored or coauthored *Sense and Humanity in Our Schools, Resource Kit for Teaching Basic Literacy in the Content Area, Units for Dynamic Teaching Program, and Profiles: A Collection of Short Biographies*, and *Vowels and Values*.

CONTENTS

1 THIS JOKER IS WILD!

Robin Williams went to college to study economics. He took a class in which the students had to $\boxed{improvise}$ speeches. He enjoyed using his imagination and speaking without notes. He felt he had discovered the thing he "was meant to do."

Williams dropped out of college. He became a stand-up comic. This led to a small role on the television show "Happy Days." People loved the wild character he played. Soon, Williams had a show of his own called "Mork and Mindy."

After conquering television, Williams moved his $\boxed{career}$ to films. His first movies were $\boxed{disappointing.}$ Williams's magic didn't seem to work on film. He was under control and seemed $\boxed{clumsy.}$ Then Williams agreed to do *Good Morning, Vietnam*. This film's writers used a trick from "Mork and Mindy." They allowed Williams to improvise his lines. That was all Williams needed. He $\boxed{created}$ original comic routines as he went along! The result was a successful movie.

Williams went on to star in such hit movies as *Dead Poet's Society*, *Awakenings*, *The Fisher King*, *Hook*, and *Mrs. Doubtfire*. With each role, he has grown as an actor. In his early movies, he was $\boxed{nervous}$ in front of the movie cameras. Then he learned how to use the cameras to his $\boxed{benefit.}$ One of Williams's most popular roles is one in which he is never seen on $\boxed{screen.}$ He is the voice of the genie in the animated movie *Aladdin*. As with "Mork and Mindy," he improvised many of his lines. His $\boxed{energy}$ helped to make the movie a big hit. Today, Williams is $\boxed{respected}$ for his comic ability.

UNDERSTANDING THE STORY

>>>> *Circle the letter next to each correct statement.*

1. Robin Williams is known for his
   a. ability to improvise.
   b. constant comedy writing.
   c. early film successes.
2. Audiences probably enjoy Williams because
   a. he is never sad.
   b. they don't know what he might do next.
   c. he makes fun of them.

MAKE AN ALPHABETICAL LIST

>>>> *Here are the ten vocabulary words in the lesson. Write them in alphabetical order in the spaces below.*

career	nervous	screen	respected	disappointing
improvise	clumsy	energy	created	benefit

1. _____

2. _____

3. _____

4. _____

5. _____

6. _____

7. _____

8. _____

9. _____

10. _____

WHAT DO THE WORDS MEAN?

>>>> *Following are some meanings, or definitions, for the ten vocabulary words in this lesson. Write the words next to their definitions.*

1. _____ uneasy; uncomfortable

2. _____ a surface or area on which movies or television images are shown

3. _____ invented

4. _____ admired

5. _____ not graceful

6. _____ not satisfying

7. _____ occupation; work

8. _____ to make up

9. _____ enthusiasm; an inner power or ability

10. _____ advantage

COMPLETE THE SENTENCES

>>>> *Use the vocabulary words in this lesson to complete the following sentences. Use each word only once.*

career	nervous	screen	respected	disappointing
improvise	clumsy	energy	created	benefit

1. Williams seems relaxed today, but cameras still make him _____.

2. Williams's _____ includes live appearances, television, and films.

3. Williams's first films were _____ to his fans.

4. In his first films, Willliams was _____ in front of the camera.

5. Mork was _____ by scriptwriters on "Happy Days."

6. Williams never actually appears on _____ in the movie *Aladdin*.

7. Williams likes to _____ his own comedy routines in comedy clubs.

8. He has learned to use movie cameras to his own _____.

9. He has so much _____ that he seems wild and out of control.

10. Williams is _____ because he works so hard.

USE YOUR OWN WORDS

>>>> *Look at the picture. What words come into your mind other than the ten vocabulary words used in this lesson? Write them on the lines below. To help you get started, here are two good words:*

1. _____ headphones _____
2. _____ talking _____
3. _____
4. _____
5. _____
6. _____
7. _____
8. _____
9. _____
10. _____

IDENTIFY THE SYNONYMS AND ANTONYMS

>>>> There are six vocabulary words listed below. To the right of each is either a synonym or an antonym. Remember: a **synonym** is a word that means the same or nearly the same as another word. An **antonym** is a word that means the opposite of another word.

>>>> *On the line beside each pair of words, write S for synonyms or A for antonyms.*

1. **disappointing**	pleasing	1. _____
2. **clumsy**	awkward	2. _____
3. **created**	destroyed	3. _____
4. **nervous**	calm	4. _____
5. **respected**	admired	5. _____
6. **benefit**	advantage	6. _____

COMPLETE THE STORY

>>>> Here are the ten vocabulary words for this lesson:

career	nervous	screen	respected	disappointing
improvise	clumsy	energy	created	benefit

>>>> *There are five blank spaces in the story below. Five vocabulary words have already been used in the story. They are underlined. Use the other five words to fill in the blanks.*

Robin Williams is always entertaining. He is never _____. He likes to improvise comedy routines on every subject. Williams seems to love working live. The eager audience doesn't make him nervous. In fact, he seems to draw his _____ from audience support. He gets wilder and wilder as they cheer. His work seems to benefit from their encouragement.

Williams loves working live. He still likes to surprise audiences. However, he has been in both television and films in his _____, too. His work is respected, but it was not always a success. At first, people were not sure about his films. The camera made Williams seem _____. He seemed unsure about what to do. Most people preferred his live comedy. They did not like the serious characters he played on the _____. He seems unworried. He has created a secure place for his work.

6

Learn More About Being Funny

>>>> *On a separate piece of paper or in your notebook or journal, complete one or more of the activities below.*

Building Language

Think of three jokes you might know in another language. Now, translate them into English. Tell them to a friend in English. Did the friend think they were funny? Write whether the jokes were funny in English. If your friend did not think they were funny, try to explain why the joke did not translate well into English.

Broadening Your Understanding

Robin Williams is known as a brilliant stand-up comic. In a stand-up routine, a comedian strings together a series of jokes. Often, the jokes have to do with things that happen to people in real life. Write your own three-minute stand-up comedy routine. Then try it out on a friend.

Extending Your Reading

Why would someone want to be a comedian? Read one of the following books to find out what causes a person to try for a career in comedy. Then write about why you would or wouldn't want a career as a comedian.

Will Rogers, by Liz Sonneborn
Bill Cosby, by George H. Hill
Eddie Murphy, by Deborah Wilburn
Whoopi Goldberg, by Mary Agnes Adams

It is cool and quiet. The ground is far below. You are slowly floating through the air. You are in a giant **helium** balloon. Balloons are the oldest form of flying machine.

In early times, balloons were made of silk. These balloons were **inflated** with hot air. To make the air hot, a small fire was built in a special stove in the **gondola.** The gondola, or basket, was hung from the balloon by ropes. People rode in the gondola.

Ballasts, or weights made of sand-filled bags, held the balloon down. When enough ballasts were taken off, the balloon rose in the air. Pilots had to avoid **ascending** too rapidly because the balloon could **rupture.** This rapid ascent would cause all the hot, light air to escape. The gondola would crash to the ground. When the balloon was **aloft,** fire was a constant **threat.**

How about coming down? Simple—the fire was put out. As the air in the balloon cooled, the balloon came down. The pilot had to **descend** slowly. If the balloon came down too fast, the gondola could be smashed. Early balloonists were both **bold** and skillful.

UNDERSTANDING THE STORY

>>>> *Circle the letter next to each correct statement.*

1. The main purpose of this story is to describe
   a. the different kinds of balloons available.
   b. how a hot-air balloon works.
   c. the very first flight made in a balloon.

2. Though it doesn't say so, from the story you get the idea that
   a. there were many accidents when balloons were first used.
   b. a person needed a license to fly a balloon.
   c. balloons were first flown in the United States.

MAKE AN ALPHABETICAL LIST

>>>> *Here are the ten vocabulary words in the lesson. Write them in alphabetical order in the spaces below.*

helium	inflated	gondola	ballasts	ascending
rupture	aloft	threat	bold	descend

1. _____

2. _____

3. _____

4. _____

5. _____

6. _____

7. _____

8. _____

9. _____

10. _____

WHAT DO THE WORDS MEAN?

>>>> *Following are some meanings, or definitions, for the ten vocabulary words in this lesson. Write the words next to their definitions.*

1. _____ gas used to fill balloons

2. _____ filled up

3. _____ a car or basket hung under a balloon

4. _____ weights used to make a gondola heavier

5. _____ going up

6. _____ to break open; to burst

7. _____ high; above the earth

8. _____ something dangerous that might happen

9. _____ to go down

10. _____ not afraid of danger; brave

COMPLETE THE SENTENCES

>>>> Use the vocabulary words in this lesson to complete the following sentences. Use each word only once.

ballasts	helium	descend	inflated	bold
rupture	ascending	threat	gondola	aloft

1. Because _____ is lighter than air, it keeps the balloon aloft.
2. The excited riders in the _____ waved at the people below.
3. The danger in _____ too rapidly is that the balloon might burst.
4. A person had to be _____ and skillful to take a balloon out in the early days because ballooning was so dangerous.
5. Sand-filled bags called _____ are released to allow the balloon to rise.
6. A balloon must _____ slowly if the landing is going to be smooth.
7. Fire was a constant _____ to the safety of the early balloonists.
8. When you are _____ in a balloon, you can see towns many miles away.
9. Children used to gather to watch the balloons being _____ before a trip.
10. The pilot became worried when she noticed a small _____ in the balloon.

USE YOUR OWN WORDS

>>>> Look at the picture. What words come into your mind other than the ten vocabulary words used in this lesson? Write them on the lines below. To help you get started, here are two good words:

1. _____ sky _____
2. _____ ground _____
3. _____
4. _____
5. _____
6. _____
7. _____
8. _____
9. _____
10. _____

UNSCRAMBLE THE LETTERS

▶▶▶▶ *Each group of letters contains the letters in one of the vocabulary words for this lesson. Can you unscramble them? Write your answers in the lines to the right of each letter group.*

Scrambled Words   **Vocabulary Words**

1. ulihem   _____
2. gsadicnen   _____
3. folta   _____
4. laltasbs   _____
5. eruturp   _____
6. dalogon   _____
7. lafindet   _____
8. dolb   _____
9. rathet   _____
10. secdned   _____

COMPLETE THE STORY

▶▶▶▶ Here are the ten vocabulary words for this lesson:

helium	ballasts	gondola	aloft	inflated
threat	bold	ascending	descent	rupture

▶▶▶▶ *There are five blank spaces in the story below. Five vocabulary words have already been used in the story. They are underlined. Use the other five words to fill in the blanks.*

Going up in a balloon is great fun for some people. You step into the _____. Ballasts are dropped, and you begin to go _____. Once _____, you can see the ground far below. In the old days, you had to be a bold person to try ballooning. There was always the threat of fire. Care had to be taken not to rupture the delicate balloon skin. When you were ready to _____, you would put out the fire. Today balloons are inflated with _____.

Learn More About Flying Machines

>>>> *On a separate piece of paper or in your notebook or journal, complete one or more of the activities below.*

Learning Across the Curriculum

Read about the science behind the flying machines that people use today. Write an explanation of how a hot air balloon, a plane, or a helicopter flies. You may want to use diagrams in your report.

Broadening Your Understanding

The Albuquerque International Balloon Fiesta in October is the biggest gathering of hot-air balloons in the United States. Every year, more than 500 hot-air balloons and their owners participate. Another 1.5 million people come to the nine-day program. Write to the Balloon Fiesta at 8309 Washington Place NE, Albuquerque, New Mexico 87113, and ask for information about the festival. Then plan a trip there, using guidebooks if you need to. Include where you will stay, how long you will stay, what you will do every day, and how much the trip will cost.

Extending Your Reading

Use one of the following books to help you make a kite. After you make your kite, be sure it flies. Then write the scientific reasons why your kite stays in the air.

Making Kites, by David Michael
Dynamite Kites, by Jack Wiley and Suzanne L. Cheatle
Better Kite Flying, by Ross Olney
Kites for Kids, by Burton and Rita Marks

Do you picture *senior* citizens sitting in rocking chairs and sharing memories? Well, hold on to that rocker because the *National* Senior Olympics will change your mind. The first senior games were held about 20 years ago in Los Angeles, California, but in 1987, the United States National Senior Olympics organized a *biennial* event. *Competitors* must be more than 55 years old and *qualify* by competing in local *contests.*

In 1989, there were about 3,500 athletes from 47 states, Puerto Rico, and three *foreign* countries. They participated in 14 sports, from archery to volleyball. The oldest man was 91, and the oldest woman was 87.

One competitor got an early start. He rode his bicycle more than 1,000 miles to reach the games in St. Louis, Missouri. Of course, he was only 64! Foot races seem to bring out the best in these athletes. One racer, who is 79 and blind, says, "I love the excitement and the people." Another competitor is a 64-year-old nun. She raced in her *habit,* with her rosary beads swinging in time to her *stride.* She took up ice skating at 52 and plans to practice the *javelin* throw next because she discovered at a recent meet that she has a natural talent for it. Forget the rocking chair. You'd better keep in shape if you want to keep up with these golden agers!

UNDERSTANDING THE STORY

>>>>> *Circle the letter next to each correct statement.*

1. The main idea of this story is that
   a. Olympic games are very challenging.
   b. senior citizens can lead very active lives.
   c. people like to travel to compete in the games.

2. The fact that 3,500 people participated in the Senior Olympics tells you that
   a. younger athletes should try to help these senior citizens.
   b. we need to build many new sports stadiums.
   c. many senior citizens are interested in keeping in shape.

MAKE AN ALPHABETICAL LIST

 Here are the ten vocabulary words in the lesson. Write them in alphabetical order in the spaces below.

senior	contests	national	foreign	biennial
habit	competitors	stride	qualify	javelin

1. _____   6. _____

2. _____   7. _____

3. _____   8. _____

4. _____   9. _____

5. _____   10. _____

WHAT DO THE WORDS MEAN?

Following are some meanings, or definitions, for the ten vocabulary words in this lesson. Write the words next to their definitions.

1. _____ having to do with a whole country

2. _____ coming from another country

3. _____ older; more than age 55

4. _____ organized sports events

5. _____ an outfit worn by a nun

6. _____ happening every two years

7. _____ a step or style of walking

8. _____ to prove oneself worthy

9. _____ a spear used in sports events

10. _____ people who play in a contest or game

16

>>>> *Use the vocabulary words in this lesson to complete the following sentences. Use each word only once.*

senior	contests	national	foreign	biennial
habit	competitors	stride	qualify	javelin

1. The original Olympics were athletic _____ in Greece thousands of years ago.

2. These were _____ games in which only Greeks could compete.

3. The _____ were the finest athletes from each city in Greece.

4. Later, there were some _____ contestants, but most were Greek.

5. An athlete trained carefully to _____ for these Olympic games.

6. Contestants threw the _____ and boxed, among other events.

7. A special _____ helped runners complete the long and difficult marathon.

8. The original Olympics were not _____ events; they were held every four years, as modern Olympics are.

9. Of course, _____ citizens did not participate in these athletic games.

10. On the other hand, Greek athletes didn't have to compete wearing a nun's _____.

USE YOUR OWN WORDS

>>>> *Look at the picture. What words come into your mind other than the ten vocabulary words used in this lesson? Write them on the lines below. To help you get started, here are two good words:*

1. _____ excited _____
2. _____ healthy _____
3. _____
4. _____
5. _____
6. _____
7. _____
8. _____
9. _____
10. _____

FIND THE ANTONYMS

>>>> **Antonyms** are words that are opposite in meaning. For example, *good* and *bad* are antonyms.

>>>> **Here are antonyms for six vocabulary words. See if you can identify the vocabulary words and write them in the spaces on the left.**

Vocabulary Words	Antonyms
1. _____	native
2. _____	fail
3. _____	young
4. _____	local
5. _____	partnerships
6. _____	helpers

COMPLETE THE STORY

>>>> Here are the ten vocabulary words for this lesson:

senior	contests	national	foreign	biennial
competitors	stride	habit	qualify	javelin

>>>> **There are five blanks in the story below. Five vocabulary words have already been used in the story. They are underlined. Use the other five words to fill in the blanks.**

How do _____ citizens know that older people like themselves can take part in these Olympics? Well, every two years, there is <u>biennial</u> publicity. Also, local _____ encourage older people to become <u>competitors</u>. To go to the _____ games, such as those in St. Louis, athletes have to _____ by winning local events. Of course, there are always some <u>foreign</u> athletes from other countries.

You don't have to do it the hard way. You can wear warm-up suits instead of a nun's <u>habit</u>. You can practice your <u>stride</u> for races a little bit at a time. You can learn how to hold the _____ before you try to throw it. The important thing to work on is the spirit of friendly competition at these games.

Learn More About Older Americans

>>>> *On a separate piece of paper or in your notebook or journal, complete one or more of the activities below.*

Learning Across the Curriculum

Scientists are making discoveries every day about how we can live longer and healthier lives. Read about some of these discoveries. Write ten guidelines that anyone can follow to help them live a longer and healthier life.

Broadening Your Understanding

Imagine you have to find sponsors for the Senior Olympics. Think about what company would benefit by supporting the Senior Olympics. Then write a letter designed to interest a likely sponsor. Explain what the program is and why getting involved with it will help the sponsor, as well as the Senior Olympics.

Extending Your Reading

The following books contain biographies of people who have succeeded. Read one of them and report on what three or four of these people accomplished when they were older.

Great Lives, by William Jay Jacobs
Women of Courage, by Dorothy Nathan
People Who Make a Difference, by Brent Ashabranner

There is a city in Europe that does not have a paved street. It does not have one made of dirt. There are no cars. No subways. No four-wheel-drive buses. The name of the city is Venice.

More than 1,000 years ago, this city was **erected** on many small **islands.** The islands are in Italy in the Adriatic Sea. Waterways are the streets and avenues of the city. They are called **canals.** These canals are filled with **gondolas,** just as your streets are filled with cars. Traffic jams are everywhere. There is very little traffic noise, no horns, and no screeching stops. You can talk with someone across a canal.

The gondolas hold two to four **passengers.** The driver, or gondolier, stands on a deck at the back of the gondola. He rows, or moves, the boat with a long oar. Some people **prefer** the larger, less expensive **water-bus.** This vehicle is a motor-driven boat. It makes **scheduled** stops along the larger canals.

With all these boats moving through the busy canals, traffic must be **regulated.** There are no stoplights and no stop signs at corners. Traffic police ride around in police boats. They even give out traffic **tickets.**

Can you imagine getting a ticket? You just broke the speed limit of 5 miles per hour!

UNDERSTANDING THE STORY

 Circle the letter next to each correct statement.

1. Gondolas are more popular with tourists than the less expensive water-bus because
   a. gondoliers are friendlier than the driver of the water-bus.
   b. gondolas are an important part of the charm of Venice.
   c. all visitors to Venice have a lot of money to spend.

2. It is possible to get a traffic ticket in Venice if
   a. your gondola doesn't have parking lights.
   b. you carry more than four passengers in your gondola.
   c. you ignore the stoplights.

MAKE AN ALPHABETICAL LIST

>>>> *Here are the ten vocabulary words in the lesson. Write them in alphabetical order in the spaces below.*

erected	islands	canals	gondolas	passengers
prefer	water-bus	scheduled	regulated	tickets

1. _____   6. _____

2. _____   7. _____

3. _____   8. _____

4. _____   9. _____

5. _____   10. _____

WHAT DO THE WORDS MEAN?

>>>> *Following are some meanings, or definitions, for the ten vocabulary words in this lesson. Write the words next to their definitions.*

1. _____ long narrow boats with a high peak at each end

2. _____ notices you get from a police officer for breaking the law

3. _____ built; constructed

4. _____ kept in working order; controlled

5. _____ bodies of land surrounded by water

6. _____ happening at definite times

7. _____ people who travel in a bus, boat, train, or plane

8. _____ waterways used like roads

9. _____ to want one thing instead of another

10. _____ a canal boat with a motor that carries many passengers

COMPLETE THE SENTENCES

>>>> *Use the vocabulary words in this lesson to complete the following sentences. Use each word only once.*

islands	scheduled	prefer	regulated	gondolas
canals	passengers	erected	water-bus	tickets

1. The water-bus makes _____ stops, but the gondolas do not.

2. We took the _____ because we were in a hurry and low on money.

3. People hire _____ when they want a slow, quiet tour of the city.

4. The _____ in different boats waved to each other.

5. Venice is made up of many small _____ connected by a series of waterways.

6. Though the water-bus costs less, most people _____ to ride in the gondolas because they are more graceful.

7. In Venice, many statues have been _____ to honor important citizens.

8. To avoid getting _____, the water-bus driver obeys the traffic rules.

9. The gondolas in Venice are just as carefully _____ as taxicabs are in other cities.

10. It is a shame to see litter floating in the _____.

USE YOUR OWN WORDS

>>>> *Look at the picture. What words come into your mind other than the ten vocabulary words used in this lesson? Write them on the lines below. To help you get started, here are two good words:*

1. _____ buildings _____
2. _____ water _____
3. _____
4. _____
5. _____
6. _____
7. _____
8. _____
9. _____
10. _____

WHICH WORD IS NOT A SYNONYM?

>>>> A **synonym** is a word that means the same as another word.

>>>> *Below are six vocabulary words. They are followed by four other words or phrases. Three are synonyms; one is not. Circle the word or phrase that is **not a synonym**.*

Vocabulary Words		Synonyms		
1. **erected**	built	constructed	destroyed	created
2. **regulated**	controlled	ordered	governed	not uniform
3. **prefer**	dislike	favor	choose	like better
4. **gondolas**	boats	autos	watercraft	vessels
5. **passengers**	riders	travelers	operators	persons who ride
6. **canals**	waterways	streets of water	watercourses	roadways

COMPLETE THE STORY

>>>> Here are the ten vocabulary words for this lesson:

erected	islands	gondolas	passengers	prefer
water-bus	scheduled	canals	regulated	tickets

>>>> *There are five blank spaces in the story below. Five vocabulary words have already been used in the story. They are underlined. Use the other five words to fill in the blanks.*

Venice is an old city. The first buildings were _____ more than 1,000 years ago. Its canals are famous in song and story. But every spring, floods overflow the waterways. This water could someday destroy the _____ of Venice. Every hundred years, Venice sinks about a foot into the Adriatic Sea. The dirt and smoke from nearby factories are also harming its buildings. This pollution must be _____ to save Venice.

Once, there were 10,000 gondolas. Now, there are less than 300. The people prefer the cheaper _____. Venice's biggest business today comes from the _____ whose tickets let them off scheduled cruise ships and planes to see the sights.

Learn More About Venice

>>>> *On a separate piece of paper or in your notebook or journal, complete one or more of the activities below.*

Building Language

All languages contain idioms, or figures of speech, that are unique to them. Look up words in English that are "borrowed" from Italian. Write them down and explain what they mean.

Learning Across the Curriculum

Venice is celebrated for its art and artists. Research some of this art. Make a copy of the piece of art you like best. It can be a painting, a sculpture, or even a building. Explain something about the history of the work and its artist. Then explain why you like it.

Broadening Your Understanding

Your town has suddenly become, like Venice, a city without paved streets. Instead, all the streets are waterways. Think about how life would be different in your town. Write an imaginary journal entry about a day in your life and how your everyday routine would change.

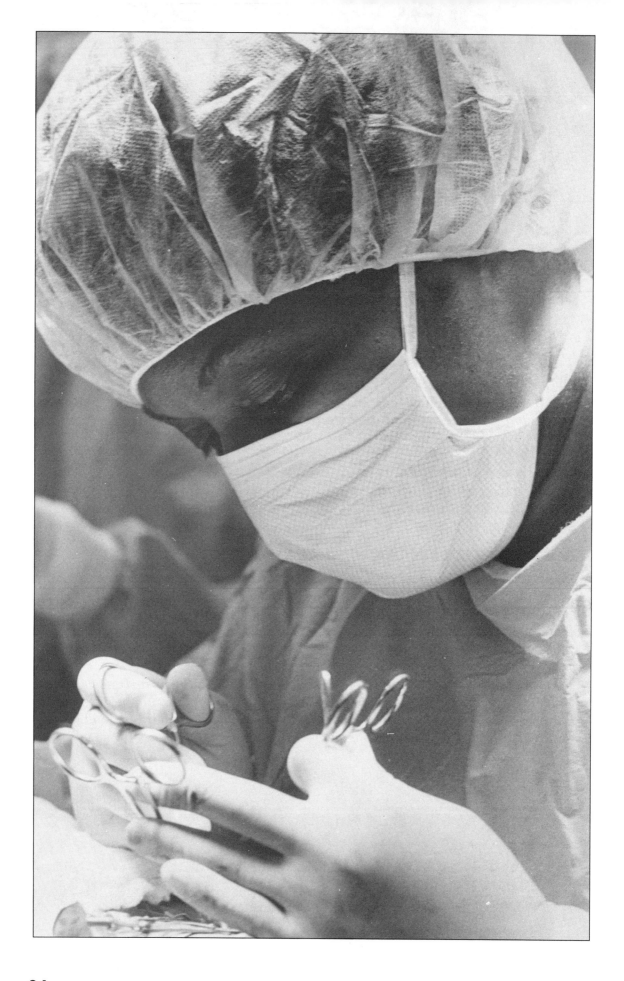

When Alexa Canady was a child, African American children had to overcome many obstacles before they could succeed. One of her elementary school teachers in Lansing, Michigan, where she was born in 1950, refused to believe Canady's test scores and lied about the results. Later, Canady's family moved to a house that was sold to them because they were African American. The seller wanted to "punish" his neighbors. Canady says, "Racism was always presented to me as *their* problem and not *our* problem."

The Civil Rights Movement of the early 1960s changed Canady's life. She was able to travel and to seek education at places that would not previously have been open to her. She says that she filled two quotas at once—she was African American and female.

 Ultimately, Canady went to medical school and then specialized in neurosurgery. She became the first African American woman neurosurgeon in the United States. There were always African American doctors. They had almost exclusively African American patients. Canady believes that this is all beginning to change. Today people of all races go to African American doctors when they need their skills.

Canady has a sense of humor, but she is saddened by the tasks still to be done. She feels that people still do not have confidence in women. She wants people to overcome their bias against African Americans and against women. Only time will tell whether she will see a society that deals properly with racial and gender prejudice.

UNDERSTANDING THE STORY

>>>> *Circle the letter next to each correct statement.*

1. Another good title for this story might be:
   a. "How to Be an African American Doctor."
   b. "A Hard Road to Success."
   c. "Some People Don't Want Success."

2. Probably, the biggest problem faced by Canady was
   a. lack of money for school.
   b. the difficulty of traveling to school.
   c. people's prejudice about African American women doctors.

MAKE AN ALPHABETICAL LIST

 Here are the ten vocabulary words in the lesson. Write them in alphabetical order in the spaces below.

obstacles	ultimately	racism	neurosurgery	movement
exclusively	previously	tasks	quotas	bias

1. _____   6. _____

2. _____   7. _____

3. _____   8. _____

4. _____   9. _____

5. _____   10. _____

WHAT DO THE WORDS MEAN?

Following are some meanings, or definitions, for the ten vocabulary words in this lesson. Write the words next to their definitions.

1. _____ barriers; difficulties

2. _____ crusade; organized effort

3. _____ operations on the brain, spinal cord, or nerves

4. _____ jobs; assignments

5. _____ earlier; before

6. _____ shares; positions held for a certain group

7. _____ a belief that one's own race is better than another's

8. _____ entirely; completely

9. _____ an unfair opinion or influence in favor of or against someone or something

10. _____ finally; at last

28

COMPLETE THE SENTENCES

>>>> *Use the vocabulary words in this lesson to complete the following sentences. Use each word only once.*

obstacles	ultimately	racism	neurosurgery	movement
exclusively	previously	tasks	quotas	bias

1. Alexa Canady completes many _____ throughout her day.
2. She thinks there are too many_____ to success for African Americans and women in America.
3. She hopes that women and African Americans _____ will be accepted as doctors.
4. Some people have a _____ against African Americans and women, but she hopes that will change.
5. The Civil Rights _____ made her education as a doctor possible.
6. Schools had _____ of African Americans, women, and other minorities to fill.
7. Canady studied _____ and practices in Detroit.
8. Discrimination does not apply _____ to African Americans or women; many other minorities are involved.
9. Today laws prevent discrimination; _____, however, minorities found it more difficult to succeed.
10. _____ means to judge people by skin color or racial characteristics.

USE YOUR OWN WORDS

>>>> *Look at the picture. What words come into your mind other than the ten vocabulary words used in this lesson? Write them on the lines below. To help you get started, here are two good words:*

1. _____ mask _____
2. _____ doctor _____
3. _____
4. _____
5. _____
6. _____
7. _____
8. _____
9. _____
10. _____

UNSCRAMBLE THE LETTERS

>>>> *Each group of letters contains the letters in one of the vocabulary words for this lesson. Can you unscramble them? Write your answers in the lines to the right of each letter group.*

Scrambled Words   **Vocabulary Words**

1. utosaq   _____
2. luyletamit   _____
3. carmis   _____
4. evenmomt   _____
5. sbai   _____
6. kstsa   _____
7. liseucyxvle   _____
8. losiprveuy   _____
9. enrouysrgeur   _____
10. slecabost   _____

COMPLETE THE STORY

>>>> Here are the ten vocabulary words for this lesson:

obstacles	ultimately	racism	neurosurgery	movement
exclusively	previously	tasks	quotas	bias

>>>> *There are five blank spaces in the story below. Five vocabulary words have already been used in the story. They are underlined. Use the other five words to fill in the blanks.*

It has not always been easy for minorities to succeed. After the <u>movement</u> for civil rights, many schools and businesses set _____ so that minorities would get a fair chance at a good job. <u>Previously</u>, people thought they did not want to work with minorities. As time passed, these people learned that their _____ was not based on fact but on their own fears. They had been guilty of _____ because they were ignorant of other races.

Of course, the _____ for minorities have not ended. There are very few minorities in <u>neurosurgery</u>. _____, people would like to see minorities in every kind of job. This work is not <u>exclusively</u> the job of minorities. We must all work to help American citizens overcome <u>obstacles</u> so they can lead better lives.

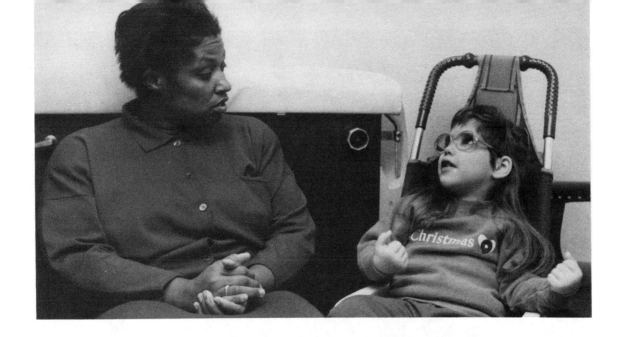

Learn More About Discrimination

>>>> *On a separate piece of paper or in your notebook or journal, complete one or more of the activities below.*

Learning Across the Curriculum

Canady says the Civil Rights Movement of the 1960s gave opportunities that helped her become a doctor. Research the Civil Rights movement. Write about the kinds of opportunties it provided for African American people in the United States.

Broadening Your Understanding

The Americans with Disabilities Act bars discrimination against persons with disabilities. The law applies to most public places, including schools. Interview the person who helps make sure this law is carried out at your school. Find out what your school has done to put the ADA into action. Then give a report to your classmates.

Extending Your Reading

Many African Americans have become scientists who made important discoveries. Read one of the following books and write a report about the scientist in whom you are most interested. Explain what he or she accomplished.

Black Pioneers of Science and Invention, by Louis Haber
Seven Black American Scientists, by Robert Hayden

The lights were **dim.** The stage was empty. The people were still. Slowly, a soft **glow** from the stage lights broke through the darkness. The **hush** of the moment was broken. The announcer's **booming** voice called out "Aretha Franklin." The crowd rose to its feet. A **celebration** was about to begin. Everyone was ready for the super sister of soul. Quietly and **elegantly** Franklin came on the stage. With the **brilliance** of a sunburst, the spotlight splashed a warm glow on the star. The dark **shadows** of the empty stage were gone. Franklin's face spread light and energy over the crowd. She moved to center stage. As the crowd roared its approval, Franklin broke into a song. Sounds of her golden voice filled the room. The warm words from "Respect" and "Natural Woman" **charmed** the crowd. Then she turned to two of her later hits, "I Can't Turn You Loose" and "Jump to It." Her version of "Amazing Grace" brought the audience to its feet once more.

The crowd's reaction was nothing new for Franklin. She has **entranced** audiences since she was a young girl. As a child, she used to sing in her father's church. Aretha performed alongside other great gospel singers. This experience had a great influence on her life. She drew upon it years later to create a unique style of singing. Her blend of gospel and blues has been popular with audiences for more than 30 years.

More recently, Franklin was featured in Whitney Houston's "How Will I Know" music video. In this video, Houston sings to Franklin the words, "I'm asking you 'cause you know about these things." This statement is a great tribute from a fellow musician.

UNDERSTANDING THE STORY

>>>> *Circle the letter next to each correct statement.*

1. The main idea of this story is that
   a. Aretha Franklin is the best singer in the business.
   b. Aretha Franklin is a very talented and well-loved singer.
   c. success does not come overnight.

2. From this story, you get the idea that
   a. Franklin has a lot to learn about playing the piano.
   b. Franklin is popular only in certain parts of the country.
   c. Franklin gives a very exciting concert.

MAKE AN ALPHABETICAL LIST

>>>> *Here are the ten vocabulary words in the lesson. Write them in alphabetical order in the spaces below.*

dim	shadows	glow	elegantly	charmed
brilliance	hush	celebration	booming	entranced

1. _____   6. _____

2. _____   7. _____

3. _____   8. _____

4. _____   9. _____

5. _____   10. _____

WHAT DO THE WORDS MEAN?

>>>> *Following are some meanings, or definitions, for the ten vocabulary words in this lesson. Write the words next to their definitions.*

1. _____ brightness; sparkle

2. _____ with a loud, deep sound

3. _____ gracefully; beautifully

4. _____ a light; to shine

5. _____ pleased and delighted

6. _____ areas of darkness or shade

7. _____ only partly lighted

8. _____ a party in honor of something

9. _____ filled with wonder

10. _____ quiet; sudden silence

COMPLETE THE SENTENCES

>>>> *Use the vocabulary words in this lesson to complete the following sentences. Use each word only once.*

celebration	brilliance	entranced	booming	hush
elegantly	dim	glow	shadows	charmed

1. When the house lights became _____, it meant that the concert was about to begin.

2. Because she was in the _____, I couldn't see the star's face.

3. With a sudden _____, the spotlight lighted up the whole stage.

4. Franklin _____ walked on the stage wearing a white sparkling gown.

5. I was so _____ by the show, I never took my eyes off the stage.

6. A soft _____ from the footlights gave everything a cozy feeling.

7. The _____ sound of the bass guitar filled the room.

8. The concert felt like a _____ of life and happiness.

9. Franklin's voice seemed to _____ the audience into silence.

10. As the last note faded away, the audience remained _____ by what they had heard.

USE YOUR OWN WORDS

>>>> *Look at the picture. What words come into your mind other than the ten vocabulary words used in this lesson? Write them on the lines below. To help you get started, here are two good words:*

1. _____ gown _____
2. _____ microphone _____
3. _____
4. _____
5. _____
6. _____
7. _____
8. _____
9. _____
10. _____

>>>> Do you remember what a **synonym** is? It is a word that means the same or nearly the same as another word. *Sad* and *unhappy* are synonyms.

>>>> *Six of the vocabulary words for this lesson are listed below. To the right of each word are three other words. Two of them are synonyms for the vocabulary word. Draw a circle around the two synonyms for each vocabulary word.*

Vocabulary Words		**Synonyms**	
1. **celebration**	festival	election	party
2. **booming**	colorful	loud	powerful
3. **elegantly**	gracefully	plainly	beautifully
4. **hush**	stillness	quiet	strength
5. **charm**	fool	please	delight
6. **dim**	sunny	dull	dark

COMPLETE THE STORY

>>>> Here are the ten vocabulary words for this lesson:

brilliance	elegantly	hush	glow	charmed
dim	entranced	booming	celebration	shadows

>>>> *There are five blank spaces in the story below. Five vocabulary words have already been used in the story. They are underlined. Use the other five words to fill in the blanks.*

Aretha Franklin did not become a star overnight. Very few people do. When she was a girl, she sang in her father's church. Even then, people knew she was special. A _____ would come over the church members when Franklin started to sing. With the _____ of sunlight through an open window, her voice would ring out. She charmed everyone. They all said that someday the whole world might be entranced by her voice.

Today, when the lights _____ and the announcer's booming voice calls out her name, a celebration begins. From out of the shadows, an _____ dressed woman walks on stage. The crowd stands and applauds wildly. With the soft, warm _____ of the footlights on her face, Franklin throws kisses to the audience and begins to sing. She is certainly a star now.

36

Learn More About Soul Music

>>>> *On a separate piece of paper or in your notebook or journal, complete one or more of the activities below.*

Appreciating Diversity

Some African Americans say that soul music reflects their heritage. Think about music you have listened to from other cultures. Borrow several tapes or CDs from a local library and listen to them. Research how this music reflects a particular culture. Share your information and any recordings with your classmates.

Learning Across the Curriculum

Listen to some recordings of soul music. Some well-known artists are James Brown, Ray Charles, Otis Redding, and Muddy Waters. Write about how the music makes you feel. Write what you think its origins may be. Then look up the definition of soul music and compare it with your guess.

Broadening Your Understanding

Soul food is said to reflect African American heritage as much as soul music does. Research soul food and why it was developed. Recipe books are a good resource. Find a recipe that you are interested in and make it for the class. Explain the history of the dish if you know it.

You don't have to go to Africa to see lions **roam** freely. You can see lions here in America. Many **species** of wild animals are kept in special parks. The animals are out in the open. They are not in cages.

This **concept** is not new. It was started by Paul Kruger in South Africa. He **developed** a park for wild animals more than 70 years ago. He was way ahead of his time. His idea has now been copied in the United States.

Visitors drive through these parks. They aren't **allowed** to get out of their cars. It would not be safe. People look out their windows at the different animals. Sometimes the animals come up to the cars.

Many animals' homes have been destroyed by careless people. But some people are concerned about animals. They are **interested** in those that are disappearing. These people **provide** money for national parks. The animals now have new homes. These parks may mean the **survival** of many **rare** wild animals.

UNDERSTANDING THE STORY

>>>> *Circle the letter next to each correct statement.*

1. Another good title for this story might be
   a. "Zoos Without Cages."
   b. "A Drive Through the Park."
   c. "Even Tame Animals Can Be Dangerous."

2. Many rare wild animals do well in an open park because
   a. people are not allowed in the park.
   b. they are fed special food and given special care.
   c. the surroundings are similar to the animals' natural surroundings.

MAKE AN ALPHABETICAL LIST

>>>> Here are the ten vocabulary words in the lesson. Write them in alphabetical order in the spaces below.

species	interested	allowed	visitors	provide
developed	roam	survival	concept	rare

1. _____   6. _____

2. _____   7. _____

3. _____   8. _____

4. _____   9. _____

5. _____   10. _____

WHAT DO THE WORDS MEAN?

>>>> Following are some meanings, or definitions, for the ten vocabulary words in this lesson. Write the words next to their definitions.

1. _____ let; permitted

2. _____ to move about as one pleases; to wander

3. _____ an idea; a plan

4. _____ built up; grew

5. _____ wanting to know more about something; concerned

6. _____ to give; to supply

7. _____ scarce; only a few left

8. _____ staying alive; existing

9. _____ animals that have some common characteristics or qualities

10. _____ people who visit; sightseers

COMPLETE THE SENTENCES

>>>> *Use the vocabulary words in this lesson to complete the following sentences. Use each word only once.*

roam	developed	allowed	species	visitors
interested	concept	rare	provide	survival

1. Animals that are similar in some ways belong to the same _____.

2. If you are _____ in animals, you must visit the San Diego Zoo.

3. The _____ of many rare wild animals depends on our ability to provide them with new homes.

4. A _____ type of goat lives in the Andes Mountains.

5. No one is _____ to see the newborn polar bear right away.

6. When you see animals that _____ freely, you realize how beautiful they are.

7. The _____ that a zoo does not need to have cages was started by Paul Kruger in South Africa more than 70 years ago.

8. _____ agree that this new type of park is a big improvement over the old-fashioned zoo.

9. The person who _____ this new type of park deserves our praise.

10. We must try to _____ the money needed to keep these parks open.

USE YOUR OWN WORDS

>>>> *Look at the picture. What words come into your mind other than the ten vocabulary words used in this lesson? Write them on the lines below. To help you get started, here are two good words:*

1. _____car_____
2. _____mane_____
3. _____
4. _____
5. _____
6. _____
7. _____
8. _____
9. _____
10. _____

MATCH THE ANTONYMS

>>>> An **antonym** is a word that means the opposite of another word. *Fast* and *slow* are antonyms. Match the vocabulary words on the left with the antonyms on the right.

>>>> *Write the correct letter in the space next to the vocabulary word.*

Vocabulary Words	Antonyms
1. _____ **allowed**	a. ordinary
2. _____ **rare**	b. forbidden
3. _____ **interested**	c. unconcerned
4. _____ **survival**	d. destroyed
5. _____ **developed**	e. extinction
6. _____ **provide**	f. take

COMPLETE THE STORY

>>>> Here are the ten vocabulary words for this lesson:

interested	rare	provide	visitors	roam
concept	allowed	survival	species	developed

>>>> *There are five blank spaces in the story below. Five vocabulary words have already been used in the story. They are underlined. Use the other five words to fill in the blanks.*

What's the new and different _____ of an animal park? It's one where animals are _____ to <u>roam</u> free! Many people find it more exciting to see wild animals on the loose instead of in cages. The parks _____ <u>visitors</u> with hours of fun. But while they have fun, the people learn about wildlife. Many Americans are _____ in the <u>survival</u> of <u>rare</u> _____ of animals. We can be proud that we have <u>developed</u> this kind of park here.

Learn More About Wild Animals

>>>> *On a separate piece of paper or in your notebook or journal, complete one or more of the activities below.*

Working Together

Find out from your state natural resources department or parks department the animals that are listed as endangered species in your state. Have each person in your group choose one of the animals to research. Why did it become endangered? What is being done to save it? Have each person write a one-page report about the animal and illustrate it with a picture or photograph. Put the reports together in a book for the class.

Broadening Your Understanding

Imagine you are in charge of asking people to give money to a wild animal park, a place that protects wild animals. Write a letter or design a brochure that will convince people to give money to your wild animal park.

Extending Your Reading

Read one of the following books about animals found in the wild or choose a book about a wild animal in which you are interested. Find out about one animal's habits and needs. Design the perfect park environment for your animal.

Amazing Animals of Australia, by National Geographic
Alligators, by Patricia Lauber
Bats, by Sylvia A. Johnson
Arctic Fox, by Gail LaBonte
Apes and Monkeys, by Donald R. Shile

8 DRAWING WITH WORDS

As a young girl, Nicholasa Mohr loved to draw. With a scrap of paper and a few crayons, she could enter an $\boxed{imaginary}$ world. This world was filled with space and freedom.

Mohr's real world was just the opposite of her imaginary world. Her real world was marked by $\boxed{poverty.}$ When Nicholasa was 8, her father died. She lived with her mother and six brothers in a $\boxed{cramped}$ apartment. Her mother then became ill. She died when Mohr was in high school.

Mohr also faced discrimination because she was a Puerto Rican. She learned that Puerto Rican $\boxed{females}$ were expected to get married and to have children. They were not expected to go to college or to work outside the home. It was $\boxed{ridiculous}$ for her to dream of a career as an artist!

Mohr refused to give up her dreams. She attended a high school of $\boxed{fashion}$ and $\boxed{design.}$ After high school, she continued her education in art. She worked many different jobs to $\boxed{obtain}$ enough money to travel. She went to Mexico to study the works of that country's great painters. The strong colors and bold designs of their works touched her deeply. Mohr felt that Mexican art somehow summed up her life as a Puerto Rican woman.

Upon returning home, Mohr set up an art studio. Her art began to be noticed for its unique design. A publisher asked Nicholasa to write a book about her $\boxed{experiences.}$ The result was *Nilda*, a story about a Puerto Rican girl growing up in New York City. Just like the author, the main character in the book uses her imagination to escape her $\boxed{dreary}$ surroundings.

Since *Nilda*, Mohr has written many other books about her Puerto Rican heritage. Each book has been a great success. Even as an adult, Nicholasa Mohr is still drawing—only now she uses words to create a picture of her culture!

UNDERSTANDING THE STORY

>>>> *Circle the letter next to each correct statement.*

1. The statement that best expresses the main idea of this selection is:
   a. Great works of art are found in Mexico.
   b. Artists should travel to increase their skills.
   c. A female struggled to become a successful artist.

2. From this story, you can conclude that
   a. Nicholasa Mohr is determined.
   b. Nicholasa Mohr is lonely.
   c. Nicholasa Mohr likes to travel.

MAKE AN ALPHABETICAL LIST

>>>> *Here are the ten vocabulary words in the lesson. Write them in alphabetical order in the spaces below.*

imaginary	poverty	cramped	females	ridiculous
experiences	fashion	obtain	design	dreary

1. _____
2. _____
3. _____
4. _____
5. _____

6. _____
7. _____
8. _____
9. _____
10. _____

WHAT DO THE WORDS MEAN?

>>>> *Following are some meanings, or definitions, for the ten vocabulary words in this lesson. Write the words next to their definitions.*

1. _____ girls; women

2. _____ state of being poor

3. _____ forms, colors, or details arranged in a certain way

4. _____ funny, silly

5. _____ current style of dress

6. _____ existing only in the mind or imagination; unreal

7. _____ all actions or events that make up a person's life

8. _____ gloomy; dull

9. _____ crowded; tight

10. _____ to gain possession of

COMPLETE THE Sentences

>>>> *Use the vocabulary words in this lesson to complete the following sentences. Use each word only once.*

design	fashion	ridiculous	experiences	females
poverty	cramped	obtain	imaginary	dreary

1. Nicholasa Mohr grew up in a life of _____.

2. Her family lived in a _____ apartment in New York City.

3. She escaped her _____ surroundings through her drawings.

4. Her pictures took her to an _____ world.

5. She studied _____ and design in high school.

6. She discovered that people thought Puerto Rican _____ should not have a career.

7. This idea was quite _____ to Mohr!

8. She worked hard to _____ the skills needed to become a great artist.

9. She studied the bold _____ in the works of great Mexican artists.

10. Mohr's life _____ are reflected in her art and writing.

USE YOUR OWN WORDS

>>>> *Look at the picture. What words come into your mind other than the ten vocabulary words used in this lesson? Write them on the lines below. To help you get started, here are two good words:*

1. _____ writer _____
2. _____ Puerto Rican _____
3. _____
4. _____
5. _____
6. _____
7. _____
8. _____
9. _____
10. _____

FIND THE ANTONYMS

>>>> **Antonyms** are words that are opposite in meaning. For example, *fast* and *slow* are antonyms.

>>>> *Match the vocabulary words on the left with the antonyms on the right. Write the correct letter in the space next to the vocabulary word.*

Vocabulary Words	Antonyms
1. _____ **poverty**	a. spacious
2. _____ **cramped**	b. real
3. _____ **obtain**	c. males
4. _____ **females**	d. bright
5. _____ **dreary**	e. lose
6. _____ **imaginary**	f. luxury

COMPLETE THE STORY

>>>> Here are the ten vocabulary words for this lesson:

cramped	fashion	ridiculous	experiences	imaginary
females	poverty	dreary	obtain	design

>>>> *There are five blank spaces in the story below. Five vocabulary words have already been used in the story. They are underlined. Use the other five words to fill in the blanks.*

Today Nicholasa Mohr is a successful writer. Many of her books tell the story of Puerto Rican <u>females</u>. The stories are generally set in _____ surroundings. The characters live a life of <u>poverty</u>. Mohr's books are based upon her own life _____. She, too, grew up in a <u>cramped</u> home. Her family did not have enough money to _____ fancy things.

Mohr worked hard to become a success. She did not think her dream of becoming famous was <u>ridiculous</u>. She studied _____ and <u>design</u> in high school. She attended special art classes. She went to Mexico to study the works of great artists. The hard work paid off! Today, Nicholasa Mohr is a famous author. Through much effort, her _____ world has become her real world.

Learn More About Nicholasa Mohr

>>>> *On a separate piece of paper or in your notebook or journal, complete one or more of the activities below.*

Broadening Your Understanding

Nicholasa Mohr used crayons to create an imaginary world. Make a drawing of an imaginary world that you would like to visit. On the back of your drawing, explain how your imaginary world is different from the real world.

Learning Across the Curriculum

Mohr's family moved from Puerto Rico to the United States. Use reference books to learn more about Mohr's native land. Look for information about other famous Americans who came from Puerto Rico, such as Raul Julia or Tito Puente. Share your findings in a report to your class.

Appreciating Diversity

Nicholasa Mohr traveled to Mexico to study the works of great Mexican artists. Learn more about the unique style of these painters. Find out how they used their art to express their feelings about their country. Write an art review to share your ideas about what you have learned. Display pictures of some of the artists' works to help illustrate your review.

9 A DANGEROUS JUMP

Think about the *various* ways that people get to their jobs. Some drive cars to work. Others ride trains or even walk to their jobs. Some people, however, parachute to work! These people are smokejumpers, a unique group of firefighters.

Smokejumpers make up a *division* of the U.S. Forest Service. The service set up the group about 50 years ago. Its purpose was to battle forest fires in the Rocky Mountains. The slopes of the mountains are very steep. Reaching the fires by foot is very difficult. The only way to get the firefighters to the fire is to drop them at the scene by *helicopter.* These firefighters, now called smokejumpers, parachute to their job!

Work as a smokejumper has its *risks.* Weather conditions can change suddenly. A small fire can become a wall of flames. This is exactly what happened in July 1994. A group of smokejumpers was battling a fire in the mountains of Colorado. The smokejumpers seemed to have the fire under control. Suddenly, *gusts* of wind roared through the area. The fire exploded into a firestorm. The storm of heat *advanced* at a *rate* of 100 feet per minute!

The smokejumpers raced for their lives. Some were unable to outrun the wall of fire. Others *sought* protection inside foil blankets called fire shelters. Still, 14 smokejumpers died in the fire. They died trying to find escape routes through parts of the forest that had burned.

By the next day, the fire had been *smothered.* The smokejumpers had done their job. They reviewed what had happened to make sure it would not happen again. Then they got ready for their next battle with *nature.*

UNDERSTANDING THE STORY

 Circle the letter next to each correct statement.

1. The statement that best expresses the main idea of this selection is:
   a. Smokejumping is a dangerous job.
   b. People get to work in many different ways.
   c. Parachute diving is fun.

2. From this story, you can conclude that
   a. fires rarely happen in the Rocky Mountains.
   b. it is easier to fight a fire on a calm day than on a windy day.
   c. it is very difficult to stop forest fires that burn on mountainsides.

MAKE AN ALPHABETICAL LIST

 Here are the ten vocabulary words in the lesson. Write them in alphabetical order in the spaces below.

various	nature	division	smothered	gusts
risks	sought	rate	helicopter	advanced

1. _____   6. _____

2. _____   7. _____

3. _____   8. _____

4. _____   9. _____

5. _____   10. _____

WHAT DO THE WORDS MEAN?

Following are some meanings, or definitions, for the ten vocabulary words in this lesson. Write the words next to their definitions.

1. _____ hazards; possibilities of danger

2. _____ the natural world

3. _____ section; group

4. _____ searched for; tried to find

5. _____ different kinds; more than one

6. _____ to cut off oxygen supply; suffocated

7. _____ moved forward

8. _____ measured quantity

9. _____ violent rushes; sudden outbursts

10. _____ aircraft with circular blades

COMPLETE THE SENTENCES

>>>> *Use the vocabulary words in this lesson to complete the following sentences. Use each word only once.*

gusts	sought	helicopter	smothered	risks
rate	various	division	nature	advanced

1. Smokejumpers make up a _____ of the U.S. Forest Service.

2. They reach forest fires by jumping from a _____.

3. They face many _____ when fighting forest fires.

4. In 1994, the smokejumpers _____ a fire in Colorado.

5. Sudden _____ of wind made the fire turn into a wall of flames.

6. A wall of fire _____ quickly toward the firefighters.

7. The fire moved at a _____ of 100 feet per minute.

8. The Smokejumpers _____ the safety of their fire shelters.

9. Smokejumpers use _____ techniques to put out fires.

10. They saw how _____ can sometimes be very unpredictable.

USE YOUR OWN WORDS

>>>> *Look at the picture. What words come into your mind other than the ten vocabulary words used in this lesson? Write them on the lines below. To help you get started, here are two good words:*

1. _____ courageous _____
2. _____ dedicated _____
3. _____
4. _____
5. _____
6. _____
7. _____
8. _____
9. _____
10. _____

>>>> In an **analogy**, similar relationships occur between words that are different. For example, *hammer* is to *carpentry* as *piano* is to *music*. The relationship is an object to its use. Here's another analogy: *rung* is to *ladder* as *seat* is to *chair*. In this relationship, the words show a part-to-whole relationship.

>>>> *See if you can complete the following analogies. Circle the correct word or words.*

1. **Computer** is to **communication** as **helicopter** is to
   a. airport   b. transportation   c. agriculture   d. music
2. **Splashes** are to **water** as **gusts** are to
   a. hills   b. leaves   c. waves   d. wind
3. **Buildings** are to **urban** as **trees** are to
   a. nature   b. streets   c. space   d. rivers
4. **Committee** is to **club** as **division** is to
   a. crowd   b. football   c. meetings   d. army
5. **Room deodorizer** is to **freshened** as **fire extinguisher** is to
   a. located   b. hope   c. smothered   d. flamed

COMPLETE THE STORY

>>>> Here are the ten vocabulary words for this lesson:

nature	sought	helicopter	advanced	risks
gusts	division	smothered	various	rate

>>>> *There are five blank spaces in the story below. Five vocabulary words have already been used in the story. They are underlined. Use the other five words to fill in the blanks.*

The Colorado fire of 1994 was not the first time smokejumpers lost their lives while battling <u>nature</u>. This _____ of the U.S. Forest Service also lost some members in 1949. They were fighting a forest fire in Mann Gulch, Montana. Just like the Colorado incident, this fire was along the steep slopes of the Rocky Mountains. In order to reach the blaze, the smokejumpers had to be dropped by _____ . As the firefighters <u>sought</u> to contain the fire, the wind suddenly picked up. The _____ of wind fanned the fire. Suddenly, a wall of flames <u>advanced</u> at an alarming <u>rate</u> toward the smokejumpers. Before the flames were finally <u>smothered</u>, 13 smokejumpers were killed. _____ agencies reviewed what happened at Mann Gulch that day. Changes were made in the way smokejumpers attack a fire. Yet, there are certain _____ that will always be present when fighting a fire.

Learn More About Fighting Fires

>>>> *On a separate piece of paper or in your notebook or journal, complete one or more of the activities below.*

Learning Across the Curriculum

Smokejumpers are called in to battle fires that blaze along steep mountainsides. Look at a topographical map of the United States. Identify five states that would probably need the help of smokejumpers to put out forest fires.

Broadening Your Understanding

Your school has regular fire drills to practice leaving the building in case of a fire. Think about the design of your home. What escape routes should your family use if a fire ever breaks out in your home? Talk about this with other members of your family. Then have a family fire drill to be sure everyone knows the best way of leaving your home.

Learning Across the Curriculum

The forest fires that occurred in Colorado and Montana were started when lightning struck a dry area of ground. However, many forest fires begin because of the mistakes humans make. Make a list of things people can do to prevent forest fires. Select one item on your list to use for a poster on fire safety.

"I don't like the sound of my voice. Nor was I ever a professional athlete." Not many TV sports **announcers** would dare say that. But Bryant Gumbel did. He's very **honest**. Maybe that is why he is considered one of the best in his **field**.

Gumbel's first job in television was at a station in Los Angeles. He was the sports announcer for the weekend games. The station asked him to change his name. They thought that Gumbel sounded too much like **mumble** and **bumble**. But he refused. He took **pride** in being honest, even about his name.

Three years later, NBC in New York wanted him. He became a **key** person on the "Grandstand" show. Before long, he was the **host** for other National Football League shows. He did the shows before, between, and after the games. This isn't an easy job. No matter how many different things may be happening off camera, the on-camera announcer must look cool and calm. He or she must also make the reports interesting. Gumbel says, "The trick is not to give one audience the same information twice." This comment means that the announcer must have many different things to say.

People like Gumbel's **style**. He was very popular as a guest on the "Today" show. It wasn't long before NBC asked him to be one of the hosts of the show. Many people consider this to be one of the top jobs in television. When people say that to Gumbel, he just smiles and says he was lucky. There's that **appealing** honesty again.

UNDERSTANDING THE STORY

>>>> *Circle the letter next to each correct statement.*

1. The main idea of this story is that
   a. sports announcing is a difficult job.
   b. Bryant Gumbel is a lucky person.
   c. Gumbel's honest style has brought him success.

2. Though it doesn't say so, from the story you can tell that
   a. many people would like to host the "Today" show.
   b. Gumbel had many other jobs before he broke into television.
   c. Gumbel plays football in his spare time.

MAKE AN ALPHABETICAL LIST

>>>> *Here are the ten vocabulary words in the lesson. Write them in alphabetical order in the spaces below.*

honest	announcers	pride	key	host
field	mumble	style	appealing	bumble

1. _____
2. _____
3. _____
4. _____
5. _____

6. _____
7. _____
8. _____
9. _____
10. _____

WHAT DO THE WORDS MEAN?

>>>> *Following are some meanings, or definitions, for the ten vocabulary words in this lesson. Write the words next to their definitions.*

1. _____ to speak in an unclear way with the lips not open enough

2. _____ people who introduce or tell about the action on TV or radio shows

3. _____ the type of job one does

4. _____ the main announcer on a show; someone giving a party for invited guests

5. _____ to act in a clumsy way

6. _____ a way of doing things

7. _____ most important; central

8. _____ truthful; not phony

9. _____ good feelings about yourself; self-respect

10. _____ likable; pleasing

COMPLETE THE SENTENCES

>>>> *Use the vocabulary words in this lesson to complete the following sentences. Use each word only once.*

announcers	field	key	appealing	pride
bumble	honest	host	mumble	style

1. Bryant Gumbel takes _____ in who he is and what he does.

2. Like many other TV _____, he reported on sports events.

3. People said that they liked his _____, or way of doing things.

4. There is something very _____ about his down-to-earth, friendly ways.

5. Before long, he was asked to be the _____ of a popular TV show.

6. Very quickly, he had become one of the best in his _____.

7. He had to be careful not to _____ if he wanted people to understand what he was saying.

8. If he were to _____ through every report, he would be laughed right out of the business.

9. Because Gumbel was the _____ person on "Grandstand," he had to be present for every show.

10. Gumbel would agree that it pays to be _____ rather than phony.

USE YOUR OWN WORDS

>>>> *Look at the picture. What words come into your mind other than the ten vocabulary words used in this lesson? Write them on the lines below. To help you get started, here are two good words:*

1. _____ speaking _____
2. _____ tie _____
3. _____
4. _____
5. _____
6. _____
7. _____
8. _____
9. _____
10. _____

CIRCLE THE SYNONYMS

>>>> Do you remember what a **synonym** is? It is a word that means the same or nearly the same as another word. *Sad* and *unhappy* are synonyms.

>>>> *Six of the vocabulary words for this lesson are listed below. To the right of each word are three words or phrases. Two of them are synonyms for the vocabulary word. Draw a circle around the two synonyms for each vocabulary word.*

Vocabulary Words		*Synonyms*	
1. **honest**	truthful	handy	sincere
2. **key**	loud	most important	essential
3. **field**	line of work	specialty	neighborhood
4. **appealing**	attractive	lazy	likable
5. **style**	hope	manner	approach
6 **host**	announcer	guest	master of ceremonies

COMPLETE THE STORY

>>>> Here are the ten vocabulary words for this lesson:

announcers	field	honest	pride	bumble
style	host	key	mumble	appealing

>>>> *There are five blank spaces in the story below. Five vocabulary words have already been used in the story. They are underlined. Use the other five words to fill in the blanks.*

You may have noticed that people who take _____ in themselves are often very <u>appealing</u> to others. Bryant Gumbel is one of these people. He didn't let the fact that his last name rhymes with _____ and <u>bumble</u> bother him. He knew that sports _____ tell people who are not actually at a sports event what they need to know. For this reason, Gumbel knew that being <u>honest</u> was the best thing he could do. He was right. Many people like him because they feel that they can trust him. They like his _____, or way of doing things. He is also interesting to listen to and seems like someone you would like to know. These qualities make him a good television news _____. It is more than luck that has made Gumbel a <u>key</u> person in his <u>field</u>.

Learn More About Broadcasting

>>>> *On a separate piece of paper or in your notebook or journal, complete one or more of the activities below.*

Building Language

Watch a sports newscast. Write down the phrases and words that you do not understand. Find out what each means and write it in a sentence. Have a friend check your work to see if you understood what each phrase or word means.

Working Together

Watch a television talk show. Then stage your own talk show with a group of people. You will need a director, a host, guests, and writers for the questions and introductions. If possible, you may want to have one student film the talk show with a video camera so the group can watch it later.

Broadening Your Understanding

Watch "60 Minutes" or another television magazine show. What kind of research must an interviewer do in order to have a successful show? Pick a person you would like to interview. Do research to come up with questions that will get the information you want. Tell your class why you are interested in interviewing this person and share with them your list of questions.

62

11 PRIMA BALLERINA

Maria Tallchief is an *accomplished* ballerina. She has brought *pleasure* to audiences around the world. *Observers* have seen her leap and glide across a stage. She can **express** her feelings in dance.

Tallchief was born in 1925 in Fairfax, Oklahoma. Her father was a Native American. When she was a *youngster,* the family moved to California. There she began her *preparation* for stardom. She studied music. She trained in ballet. Some of her teachers were famous *professional* dancers.

Tallchief was a good learner. She became a *brilliant* dancer. She was the star dancer of the New York City Ballet. She was also a *guest* with other dance companies. She became known for her great *attention* to detail.

In 1946, Tallchief married George Balanchine. He created many ballets. The two artists worked together. She danced the leading role in his ballet *The Firebird*. This role made her famous around the world.

In 1980, Tallchief started the Chicago City Ballet. She taught young dancers. She supervised the shows. Newcomers learned why she is the most brilliant American ballerina of her time.

UNDERSTANDING THE STORY

 Circle the letter next to each correct statement.

1. Maria Tallchief is known as a brilliant ballerina because she
   a. married a choreographer.
   b. is a Native American.
   c. pays great attention to detail.

2. Maria Tallchief probably
   a. wishes she could leave the world of ballet.
   b. enjoys dance even though it is hard work.
   c. would tell young ballerinas to study something else.

MAKE AN ALPHABETICAL LIST

 Here are the ten vocabulary words in the lesson. Write them in alphabetical order in the spaces below.

professional	accomplished	guest	express	brilliant
observes	youngster	preparation	pleasure	attention

1. _____
2. _____
3. _____
4. _____
5. _____

6. _____
7. _____
8. _____
9. _____
10. _____

WHAT DO THE WORDS MEAN?

Following are some meanings, or definitions, for the ten vocabulary words in this lesson. Write the words next to their definitions.

1. _____ visitor

2. _____ child

3. _____ concentration

4. _____ readiness

5. _____ having to do with earning a living in a job that requires certain skills

6. _____ viewers

7. _____ delight; enjoyment

8. _____ to make known

9. _____ splendid; magnificent

10. _____ skilled; experienced

COMPLETE THE SENTENCES

>>>> *Use the vocabulary words in this lesson to complete the following sentences. Use each word only once.*

pleasure	attention	accomplished	preparation	professional
observers	guest	express	youngster	brilliant

1. Maria Tallchief is an _____ ballerina.

2. Her _____ dance delights audiences.

3. Tallchief studied music and dance as a _____.

4. Some of her teachers were _____ dancers.

5. They taught her how to _____ emotions through dance.

6. This _____ helped Tallchief become a star.

7. She is known for paying close _____ to detail.

8. Tallchief performed as a _____ with many dance companies.

9. _____ wonder at the way Tallchief moved her body.

10. Her dance brought great _____ to all members of the audience.

USE YOUR OWN WORDS

>>>> *Look at the picture. What words come into your mind other than the ten vocabulary words used in this lesson? Write them on the lines below. To help you get started, here are two good words:*

1. _____ Native American _____
2. _____ ballerina _____
3. _____
4. _____
5. _____
6. _____
7. _____
8. _____
9. _____
10. _____

>>>> There are six vocabulary words listed below. To the right of each is either a synonym or an antonym. Remember: A **synonym** is a word that means the same or nearly the same as another word. An **antonym** is a word that means the opposite of another word.

>>>> *On the line beside each pair of words, write **S** for synonym or **A** for antonym.*

Vocabulary Words	Antonyms and Synonyms	
1. **observers**	viewers	1. _____
2. **pleasure**	disgust	2. _____
3. **youngster**	adult	3. _____
4. **brilliant**	dull	4. _____
5. **guest**	visitor	5. _____
6. **professional**	amateur	6. _____

COMPLETE THE STORY

>>>> Here are the ten vocabulary words for this lesson:

attention	accomplished	brilliant	professional	observers
youngster	preparation	pleasure	guest	express

>>>> *There are five blank spaces in the story below. Five vocabulary words have already been used in the story. They are underlined. Use the other five words to fill in the blanks.*

Maria Tallchief was a professional dancer. _____ delighted at watching her move across a stage. The movement of her body could _____ different emotions. Her dancing brought great _____ to every audience.

Tallchief worked hard on her dance. She spent long hours in preparation for a new role. She was known for her _____ to detail. Even as a youngster, she was devoted to ballet. Because of this effort, Tallchief became a brilliant dancer. She was invited to be a _____ in theaters around the world. Today Maria Tallchief is known as an accomplished American ballerina.

Learn More About Ballet

>>>> *On a separate piece of paper or in your notebook or journal, complete one or more of the activities below.*

Learning Across the Curriculum

Some ballets tell a story through dance. Write or tell a story that you think could be told without words. Write words that describe the movements of the dancers in your ballet.

Broadening Your Understanding

Two other great American ballerinas of the mid-1900s were Melissa Hayden and Nora Kaye. Use reference materials to learn about the lives of these two dancers. Then, based upon what you discover, write a Help Wanted ad for a prima ballerina. Make sure to include a description of the job, as well as job requirements.

Learning Across the Curriculum

It is believed that ballet began during the 1500s. Use reference materials to learn more about the history of this form of dance. Discover where and when the first ballet was performed. Create a poster that advertises this performance.

The captain of the fishing boat stops the engines. He looks out over the calm, clear water. A person is resting in a chair out on the deck. The mate walks over. "It's time to get ready," he says. Suddenly, you realize the person on board is . . . you!

You are about to enter a brand new world—the sea. Fish can *breathe* underwater, but people cannot. Divers must carry their own air. The captain brings over an *aqualung.* The aqualung has one or two tanks. The tanks are filled with oxygen. A rubber hose carries the oxygen to the *mouthpiece.* It is through this mouthpiece that you will breathe underwater.

You strap large *fins* to your feet. Next comes the face mask. It is made of rubber with a glass face plate. Your diving partner is dressed the same way. The captain asks if both of you are ready.

You enter the sea. Below, brightly colored *coral* looks like stone plants. Seaweed and other plants wave in the ocean current. *Schools* of tiny fish swim all around you. What's that? A shark? No, it's only a big, old grouper. These are all the true *inhabitants* of the sea. You are only a *scuba* diver.

Your experienced partner watches the time. It is passing swiftly. You don't want to run out of air. Watch your *depth* at all times. Going too deep can cause injury or death. *Surfacing* too fast can also be dangerous. All too soon, it's time to go back.

Let's do it again. But please remember: You must never dive alone.

UNDERSTANDING THE STORY

>>>> *Circle the letter next to each correct statement.*

1. Another good title for this story might be:
   a. "The True Inhabitants of the Sea."
   b. "Diving Beneath the Sea."
   c. "How to Prevent Drowning."

2. The warning "never dive alone" is probably made because
   a. it is against the law to dive alone.
   b. it is more fun to dive with a friend.
   c. a diver could run into trouble and need help.

MAKE AN ALPHABETICAL LIST

 Here are the ten vocabulary words in the lesson. Write them in alphabetical order in the spaces below.

inhabitants	schools	fins	coral	depth
breathe	aqualung	mouthpiece	scuba	surfacing

1. _____   6. _____

2. _____   7. _____

3. _____   8. _____

4. _____   9. _____

5. _____   10. _____

WHAT DO THE WORDS MEAN?

>>>> *Following are some meanings, or definitions, for the ten vocabulary words in this lesson. Write the words next to their definitions.*

1. _____ persons or animals who live in a place

2. _____ gear that allows breathing underwater; *self-contained underwater breathing apparatus*

3. _____ rubber flippers that people wear on their feet to swim and dive

4. _____ a dive tank that supplies air

5. _____ a part of the scuba equipment that the diver holds in the mouth

6. _____ to take air in and let air out

7. _____ large numbers of fish swimming together

8. _____ a hard substance made by the skeletons of tiny sea animals

9. _____ the distance from top to bottom

10. _____ coming to the top of the water

70

COMPLETE THE SENTENCES

>>>> *Use the vocabulary words in this lesson to complete the following sentences. Use each word only once.*

breathe	depth	schools	inhabitants	mouthpiece
scuba	surfacing	aqualung	fins	coral

1. _____ stands for "self-contained *u*nderwater *b*reathing *a*pparatus."

2. Since the invention of the _____, people have been able to explore the world of the sea.

3. The true _____ of the sea can breathe underwater.

4. Although _____ can be beautiful, its sharp edges can be dangerous.

5. When the diver found it difficult to _____, she signaled for help.

6. _____ of tiny green fish swam near the old shipwreck.

7. If your _____ is not firmly in place, you may swallow some water.

8. When _____, you must be careful not to come up too fast.

9. The _____ that you wear on your feet help you to swim.

10. When the diver reached a _____ of 70 feet, he decided he had gone deep enough.

USE YOUR OWN WORDS

>>>> *Look at the picture. What words come into your mind other than the ten vocabulary words used in this lesson? Write them on the lines below. To help you get started, here are two good words:*

1. _____ bubbles _____
2. _____ face mask _____
3. _____
4. _____
5. _____
6. _____
7. _____
8. _____
9. _____
10. _____

UNSCRAMBLE THE LETTERS

>>>> *Each group of letters contains the letters in one of the vocabulary words for this lesson. Can you unscramble them? Write your answers in the lines to the right of each letter group.*

Scrambled Words   **Vocabulary Words**

1. bcsua   _____
2. lcrao   _____
3. tdhpe   _____
4. lsshcoo   _____
5. hebtera   _____
6. carfinsug   _____
7. nifs   _____
8. thanbitanis   _____
9. pomiethuce   _____
10. laguquna   _____

COMPLETE THE STORY

>>>> Here are the ten vocabulary words for this lesson:

schools	inhabitants	coral	depth	fins
breathe	mouthpiece	aqualung	scuba	surfacing

>>>> *There are five blanks in the story below. Five vocabulary words have already been used in the story. They are underlined. Use the other five words to fill in the blanks.*

The world beneath the sea is beautiful but dangerous. You may learn how to be one of the part-time _____ of the sea. But special <u>scuba</u> equipment and training are needed. First, you have to have a mask, <u>fins</u>, and an _____. The <u>mouthpiece</u> of the aqualung must fit comfortably in your mouth so that you will be able to _____ underwater. There will be many lessons on how to use this equipment. You will learn to what _____ you can safely descend. The instructor will teach you <u>surfacing</u> skills. After your training, you, too, will see _____ of fish and bright <u>coral</u> on the bottom of the sea. Happy diving!

Learn More About Sea Exploration

>>>> *On a separate piece of paper or in your notebook or journal, complete one or more of the activities below.*

Learning Across the Curriculum

The Great Barrier Reef in Australia is one of the best places in the world to scuba dive. Research the Great Barrier Reef. Find out why divers travel from around the world to dive there. What is someone who dives there likely to see?

Broadening Your Understanding

Many shops that sell diving equipment are staffed by people who love to scuba dive. Call one of these shops and interview an experienced diver. Ask about his or her most memorable dive. Write a newspaper article about your findings.

Extending Your Reading

Read one of the following books about scuba diving. Pretend you are a scuba diver on a famous dive. Write about what you saw and experienced.

Swimming and Scuba Diving, by Michael Jay
Divers, by Kendall McDonald
Sport Diving, by Carole S. Briggs

Billy Crystal was raised near New York City. He worked as a teacher. Then he decided to try to go into show business. He took care of his baby daughter during the day. At night, he went into New York City to try out his act at comedy clubs. He wasn't paid, but he learned how to make people laugh. Eventually, he moved to California. There, he worked in television. He soon became better known. His skills grew, too.

Then came Crystal's big second chance. He was hired for the new season of "Saturday Night Live." On that show, he became famous for his unusual humor. The show was a perfect place for him to show off the funny characters that he can play. In a way, it's ironic that Crystal found success on the show. He was supposed to be on the original "Saturday Night Live" in 1975. At the last minute, his part was canceled. Crystal had to wait a few more years to get his shot at stardom.

Since leaving the show, Crystal has appeared in a number of hit movies. *City Slickers I* and *II* and *When Harry Met Sally* were very popular with his fans. In 1990, Crystal hosted the Academy Award ceremonies. The show was seen by nearly one billion people around the world! The viewers discovered that Billy Crystal is a very talented comedian.

UNDERSTANDING THE STORY

 Circle the letter next to each correct statement.

1. Billy Crystal was
   a. on the original "Saturday Night Live."
   b. taken off the "Saturday Night Live" show at the last moment.
   c. never on "Saturday Night Live."

2. To become a good comic,
   a. you need talent but not much practice.
   b. you shouldn't practice too much.
   c. you need both talent and plenty of practice.

MAKE AN ALPHABETICAL LIST

 Here are the ten vocabulary words in the lesson. Write them in alphabetical order in the spaces below.

characters	eventually	ironic	skills	canceled
hired	comedy	famous	fans	comedian

1. _____
2. _____
3. _____
4. _____
5. _____

6. _____
7. _____
8. _____
9. _____
10. _____

WHAT DO THE WORDS MEAN?

 Following are some meanings, or definitions, for the ten vocabulary words in this lesson. Write the words next to their definitions.

1. _____ people in stories, plays, and television shows and movies.

2. _____ something that is opposite to what you would expect

3. _____ stopped; done away with

4. _____ something funny

5. _____ people who are enthusiastic about a performer

6. _____ finally; in the end

7. _____ abilities that come from practice

8. _____ given a job

9. _____ well known by many people

10. _____ someone who tells jokes or performs in funny ways

COMPLETE THE SENTENCES

>>>> *Use the vocabulary words in this lesson to complete the following sentences. Use each word only once.*

characters	eventually	ironic	skills	canceled
hired	comedy	famous	fans	comedian

1. It took a long time, but _____ Billy Crystal became a star.

2. The show was _____ because not enough people watched it.

3. It's _____ that Crystal did so well in a show that had once dropped him.

4. Billy Crystal does many funny _____.

5. Only if you practice will you develop your _____ as a comedian.

6. He was _____ for a new season on "Saturday Night Live."

7. Some people would rather see a _____ than a serious play.

8. We were excited to see the _____ actor.

9. The _____ began to applaud the show.

10. Billy Crystal is a well-known _____.

USE YOUR OWN WORDS

>>>> *Look at the picture. What words come into your mind other than the ten vocabulary words used in this lesson? Write them on the lines below. To help you get started, here are two good words:*

1. _____ appealing _____
2. _____ humor _____
3. _____
4. _____
5. _____
6. _____
7. _____
8. _____
9. _____
10. _____

UNSCRAMBLE THE LETTERS

>>>> *Each group of letters represents one of the vocabulary words for this lesson. Can you unscramble them? Write your answers in the blanks on the right.*

Scrambled Words   **Vocabulary Words**

1. hatescracr   _____
2. niiorc   _____
3. yvelaluten   _____
4. moydce   _____
5. lcdeacne   _____
6. nfas   _____
7. uofsam   _____
8. dimconae   _____
9. eidhr   _____
10. lkslis   _____

COMPLETE THE STORY

>>>> Here are the ten vocabulary words for this lesson:

characters	eventually	ironic	skills	canceled
hired	comedy	famous	fans	comedian

>>>> *There are five blank spaces in the story below. Five vocabulary words have already been used in the story. They are underlined. Use the other five words to fill in the blanks.*

The _____ that he plays are sometimes different from the real Billy Crystal. The <u>fans</u> laugh when Crystal plays a funny single man. They can't tell that he is really a family man. Crystal is close to his children. A <u>comedian</u> is away from home a lot. Even so, Crystal's marriage is happy.

There are other things people may not see about Billy Crystal. He keeps trying. His big break on "Saturday Night Live" was <u>canceled</u>. That didn't stop him. Crystal is _____ today. But he worked hard to improve his _____. It took years before he _____ became successful. It's <u>ironic</u> that <u>comedy</u> is such hard work. Yet, it has to look easy. You don't get _____ for good jobs until being funny no longer looks like work.

Learn More About Comedians

>>>> *On a separate piece of paper or in your notebook or journal, complete one or more of the activities below.*

Building Language

Watch a stand-up comedy routine or a situation comedy on TV. List the phrases or jokes that you do not understand. Write down your guess of what the phrase or joke means as it was used. Ask a friend to check if you are right.

Learning Across the Curriculum

Comic strips often tell jokes in an effort to look at the world in a different way. Find a comic strip from a newspaper or magazine that makes a joke. Write how the comic-strip writer uses humor. Share the information with your class.

Broadening Your Understanding

Some comedy on TV is funny. Some isn't. Watch an episode of the top-rated and bottom-rated situation comedies on TV. What makes one successful and the other not? Which did you think was funnier and why? Write reviews of the two shows.

14 TOO COLD FOR COMFORT

Siberia is *bleak* and *barren.* The climate is *severe.* The winters are long. There are many blizzards. The wind blows constantly. Sometimes it reaches 100 miles per hour. The temperatures are bitter cold. The summer is short, and it's very hot.

Siberia lies in the northern part of Asia. For years, Siberia was part of the Soviet Union. Then, in 1992, this vast country split into smaller countries. Siberia became part of the Russian Federation.

More than 32 million people live in Siberia. However, there are few cities in this huge land. The towns are far apart. You can travel for days and *rarely* see anyone! Siberia's harsh climate is not good for farming. So there are few farms. However, the earth beneath the surface is rich. Iron ore, gold, silver, and other *precious* metals are mined. Oil and natural gas wells sink deep into the ground. These resources are important to the Russian *economy.*

Siberia has an unusual history. Beginning in the 18th *century,* Siberia became used as a prison *colony.* First, only criminals were sent there. Later, it became a place of *exile.* Citizens who spoke against the government were sent to work in the mines. Life in a Siberian *penal* colony usually meant an early death.

About 100 years ago, a railroad was built across Russia. This railroad helped new settlers reach Siberia. The government encouraged people to move there. They were needed to work in the mines and in the oil fields. To date, few people have moved there. Siberia may never be a land of towns and cities.

UNDERSTANDING THE STORY

 Circle the letter next to each correct statement.

1. The main idea of this story is that
   a. Siberia is best known as a prison colony.
   b. Siberia is the coldest place on earth.
   c. Siberia is bleak and barren but important to the Soviet economy.

2. Most likely, not many people have chosen to move to Siberia because
   a. the government has not offered them enough money.
   b. the riches there cannot make up for the hard life.
   c. they don't want to live among the prisoners.

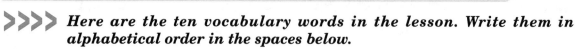

MAKE AN ALPHABETICAL LIST

>>>> *Here are the ten vocabulary words in the lesson. Write them in alphabetical order in the spaces below.*

barren	rarely	precious	economy	colony
century	exile	penal	severe	bleak

1. _____
2. _____
3. _____
4. _____
5. _____

6. _____
7. _____
8. _____
9. _____
10. _____

WHAT DO THE WORDS MEAN?

>>>> *Following are some meanings, or definitions, for the ten vocabulary words in this lesson. Write the words next to their definitions.*

1. _____ dreary; swept by winds

2. _____ money, goods, and services

3. _____ not often; seldom

4. _____ involving punishment

5. _____ a settlement or town set up by a group of people

6. _____ a forced removal from one's homeland

7. _____ having great value

8. _____ very harsh or difficult; stern

9. _____ a period of 100 years

10. _____ not producing anything; bare

COMPLETE THE SENTENCES

>>>> **Use the vocabulary words in this lesson to complete the following sentences. Use each word only once.**

precious	penal	bleak	rarely	economy
severe	exile	century	colony	barren

1. When people see the _____ landscape of Siberia, they usually wonder how anyone survives there.

2. Land that is _____ is not usually good for farming.

3. Being sent to a prison _____ was punishment for speaking out against the government.

4. People who were sent to prison colonies _____ returned to their homes.

5. Settlers were unaware that _____ metals lay beneath their feet.

6. It would have helped the Soviet _____ to make better use of the land.

7. After a _____ winter, even a short summer must feel good to the people in Siberia.

8. Siberia is thought of as a place of _____ rather than a land of promise.

9. There are very sad stories written about life in a _____ colony.

10. Over the last _____, important changes have taken place in Siberia.

USE YOUR OWN WORDS

>>>> **Look at the picture. What words come into your mind other than the ten vocabulary words used in this lesson? Write them on the lines below. To help you get started, here are two good words:**

1. _____ children _____
2. _____ coats _____
3. _____
4. _____
5. _____
6. _____
7. _____
8. _____
9. _____
10. _____

MAKE NEW WORDS FROM OLD

>>>> *Look at the vocabulary words* penal *and* economy. *Together, they are made up of 12 letters. See how many words you can form by using the letters of these words. Make up at least ten words. Write your words in the spaces below.*

penal

1. _____
2. _____
3. _____
4. _____
5. _____

economy

6. _____
7. _____
8. _____
9. _____
10. _____

COMPLETE THE STORY

>>>> Here are the ten vocabulary words for this lesson:

bleak	rarely	precious	economy	century
colony	exile	penal	severe	barren

>>>> *There are five blank spaces in the story below. Five vocabulary words have already been used in the story. They are underlined. Use the other five words to fill in the blanks.*

In the <u>century</u> before last, Russia used the area of Siberia as a _____ <u>colony</u> for criminals and political prisoners. The inhabitants of the land were mainly native Asians, Russian explorers, and prisoners. For the prisoners, it was bad enough to be forced into _____, but cold and hunger made it worse. The <u>severe</u> winters killed many of them.

Siberia is a land rich in oil, coal, and lumber, as well as silver, gold, and other <u>precious</u> metals. The government knew that this wealth was necessary for the nation's _____. But there were _____ enough Siberians to bring it out. So the government tried to encourage other citizens to go live and work in the _____ and <u>barren</u> land.

Learn More About Siberia

>>>> *On a separate piece of paper or in your notebook or journal, complete one or more of the activities below.*

Learning Across the Curriculum

Research the geography of Siberia. Write a description of the area for someone who has never heard of it and wants to travel there. Include the different kinds of land features in Siberia, its boundaries, and what the weather is like at different times of the year. Share your description with a classmate.

Broadening Your Understanding

The Trans-Siberian Railway is more than a hundred years old. Today travelers still take the train through Siberia on this route. Imagine that you are planning a trip through Siberia on the railway. Look in travel magazines and brochures and write a summary of your trip. What will you be seeing? What cities and towns will you go through? What will the highlights of the trip be?

Appreciating Diversity

Find out about the different ethnic groups that live in Siberia, such as the Tungus, Evenkis, Okrugs, and Yakuts. How have these people adapted to living in such a harsh climate? Describe how they live. Give an oral presentation to the class.

15 A DOUBLE VISION

Leo and Diane Dillon are talented artists. They use their skills to illustrate children's books. As illustrators, the Dillons design pictures to *accompany* the words of a story. These *detailed* pictures make the story come alive.

The Dillons have worked together for more than 35 years. They have a *system* for illustrating a book. The first step is reading the text of the story. Then they *discuss* ideas for pictures. Once they agree on an idea, they begin to *sketch* it out. They take turns working on the drawing. They blend their skills to create the sketch. The result is a combination of the two artists' styles.

The pictures produced by this system are interesting. *Generally,* the characters' faces seem quite real. This is because the Dillons often use real people as models for their characters. Sometimes, the artists draw themselves in their pictures. They have even *included* their pet cats in their sketches.

Through their hard work, the Dillons have gained the *admiration* of many writers. They are *constantly* asked to work on new books. However, this success did not come easily. The Dillons admit that their career has been a long, slow struggle. Yet, they never gave up. They continued to *cooperate* on ideas as a team. After 35 years of teamwork, they are enjoying the success they deserve.

UNDERSTANDING THE STORY

>>>> *Circle the letter next to each correct statement.*

1. The story shows that
   a. it is difficult to work with a partner.
   b. all artists should work in pairs.
   c. teamwork pays off.

2. From this story, you can conclude that
   a. the Dillons want to write a book.
   b. the Dillons enjoy their work.
   c. the Dillons are allergic to dogs.

MAKE AN ALPHABETICAL LIST

>>>> *Here are the ten vocabulary words in the lesson. Write them in alphabetical order in the spaces below.*

system	sketch	constantly	detailed	generally
accompany	cooperate	discuss	admiration	included

1. _____
2. _____
3. _____
4. _____
5. _____

6. _____
7. _____
8. _____
9. _____
10. _____

WHAT DO THE WORDS MEAN?

>>>> *Following are some meanings, or definitions, for the ten vocabulary words in this lesson. Write the words next to their definitions.*

1. _____ a feeling of wonder and approval

2. _____ incomplete drawing

3. _____ having many small parts

4. _____ to go along with

5. _____ to talk over

6. _____ a plan; a set of rules

7. _____ to work together

8. _____ usually; ordinarily

9. _____ made part of; involved

10. _____ repeatedly; happening again and again

COMPLETE THE SENTENCES

>>>> *Use the vocabulary words in this lesson to complete the following sentences. Use each word only once.*

generally	detailed	admiration	cooperate	constantly
accompany	sketch	included	system	discuss

1. Leo and Diane Dillon have a _____ for illustrating a book.

2. They _____ on all the work.

3. After reading the story, they _____ ideas for pictures.

4. They take turns working on a _____.

5. Their illustrations are quite _____.

6. They have _____ sketches of their cats in their illustrations.

7. The Dillons _____ use real people as models for their work.

8. Many authors want the Dillons to draw pictures to _____ their stories.

9. The Dillons are _____ asked to illustrate new books.

10. Their hard work won them the _____ of many fans.

USE YOUR OWN WORDS

>>>> *Look at the picture. What words come into your mind other than the ten vocabulary words used in this lesson? Write them on the lines below. To help you get started, here are two good words:*

1. _____ creative _____
2. _____ illustration _____
3. _____
4. _____
5. _____
6. _____
7. _____
8. _____
9. _____
10. _____

CIRCLE THE SYNONYMS

>>>> Do you remember what a **synonym** is? It is a word that means the same or nearly the same as another word. *Unhappy* and *sad* are synonyms.

>>>> *Six of the vocabulary words in this lesson are listed below. To the right of each vocabulary word are three other words or groups of words. Two of them are synonyms for the vocabulary word. Draw a circle around the two synonyms for each vocabulary word.*

Vocabulary Words		*Synonyms*	
1. **cooperate**	disagree	work together	unite
2. **system**	plan	machine	method
3. **generally**	usually	often	never
4. **constantly**	repeatedly	rarely	often
5. **discuss**	talk	be silent	speak about
6. **admiration**	hatred	wonder	respect

COMPLETE THE STORY

>>>> Here are the ten vocabulary words for this lesson:

accompany	admiration	detailed	generally	system
cooperate	discuss	included	sketch	constantly

>>>> *There are five blanks in the story below. Five vocabulary words have already been used in the story. They are underlined. Use the other five words to fill in the blanks.*

Leo and Diane Dillon _____ to illustrate children's books. They _____ follow a <u>system</u> when working on a new book. They read the book. They <u>constantly</u> come up with ideas for pictures to <u>accompany</u> the story. They _____ their ideas. They take turns working on each _____. The <u>detailed</u> drawings produced by this system are quite unique. Through their sketches, the Dillons have gained the _____ of the publishing world. Many authors want the Dillons' drawings <u>included</u> in their books.

Learn More About The Dillons

>>>> *On a separate piece of paper or in your notebook or journal, complete one or more of the activities below.*

Broadening Your Understanding

In this lesson, you discovered that Leo and Diane Dillon often use real people as models for the characters they draw. Suppose you needed to illustrate a book about a person your own age. Who would you use as a real-life model for this character? Write a brief paragraph identifying whom you would select as your model and why you chose this person.

Learning Across the Curriculum

The Dillons are quite famous for their illustrations of books based on African tales or traditions. Use reference texts to find a folktale from another culture. Share the folktale with your classmates. Make a poster that illustrates one part of the tale.

Extending Your Reading

In a library, find the books below or others illustrated by the Dillons. Look at the similarities and the differences of the Dillons' art styles used in the books. Read one of the books and write a paragraph telling how you think the Dillons' pictures help to tell the story.

Northern Lullaby, by Nancy White
The People Could Fly: American Black Folktales, by Virginia Hamilton
Many Thousand Gone, by Virginia Hamilton
Why Mosquitoes Buzz in People's Ears, by Verna Aardema
Aida, by Leontyne Price

16 THE ART OF SELF-DEFENSE

Two people come to the center of the mat. They bow. This movement shows respect for each other and for their sport. They have practiced for hours. Now, they are ready. The judges are also ready. This contest is a show of skill. This sport is karate.

Karate is a Japanese word. It means "open hand." This is because it is never violent. It is **violent** only in the movies and on TV. What is shown on TV and in movies is not true karate.

The **origin** of this art **form** is **uncertain.** Many people believe it was started by a Buddhist monk in **remote** times. He taught it in China more than 1,300 years ago. Today it has **spread** all over the world. It is taught in Japan. Many Koreans have become experts. People of the United States are studying it. Someday we may see karate included in the Olympics. Because of its true meaning, it may help people understand each other better.

Karate has three **purposes.** It develops a person's **spiritual** being. It **stimulates** the mind. It increases the body's **strength.** Karate is meant to build the mind, body, and spirit. It is used to protect life—never to destroy it.

UNDERSTANDING THE STORY

>>>> *Circle the letter next to each correct statement.*

1. The main idea of this story is that
   a. karate only exists on television or in the movies.
   b. a person must be religious to do karate.
   c. karate is a form of self-defense that has other benefits as well.

2. Though the story doesn't say so, karate, which means "open hand," probably gets its name from the fact that
   a. the object is to force the other person's open hand to the mat.
   b. hitting with an open hand is one of the main moves.
   c. a sword is held in the open hand.

MAKE AN ALPHABETICAL LIST

>>>> *Here are the ten vocabulary words in the lesson. Write them in alphabetical order in the spaces below.*

form	purpose	strength	stimulates	violent
remote	origin	spiritual	spread	uncertain

1. _____

2. _____

3. _____

4. _____

5. _____

6. _____

7. _____

8. _____

9. _____

10. _____

WHAT DO THE WORDS MEAN?

>>>> *Following are some meanings, or definitions, for the ten vocabulary words in this lesson. Write the words next to their definitions.*

1. _____ the beginning; where something comes from

2. _____ not known for sure; doubtful

3. _____ far off in time

4. _____ gone all over

5. _____ a type; a kind

6. _____ holy or religious; having to do with the soul

7. _____ power; force

8. _____ goals; aims

9. _____ excites; makes more active

10. _____ wild; roughly forceful

COMPLETE THE SENTENCES

>>>> *Use the vocabulary words in this lesson to complete the following sentences. Use each word only once.*

spread	violent	form	remote	spiritual
origin	uncertain	stimulates	strength	purposes

1. Karate is an ancient sport, surviving from _____ times.

2. The _____ of karate is not known, but it may have begun in China.

3. Karate _____ the mind and allows a person to think more clearly.

4. Karate has three _____: to build the mind, body, and spirit.

5. The art of karate _____ from China to Japan and Korea.

6. Karate is considered a _____ of art when it is done with grace and skill.

7. There is a _____, almost religious, quality to karate that people like.

8. We are _____ about the beginnings of karate, but we think it was started by a Buddhist monk.

9. Just knowing the _____ of your body has increased can make you feel safer.

10. Too often, the _____ side of karate is all that is shown on TV.

USE YOUR OWN WORDS

>>>> *Look at the picture. What words come into your mind other than the ten vocabulary words used in this lesson? Write them on the lines below. To help you get started, here are two good words:*

1. _____ sash _____
2. _____ fist _____
3. _____
4. _____
5. _____
6. _____
7. _____
8. _____
9. _____
10. _____

MATCH THE ANTONYMS

>>>> An **antonym** is a word that means the opposite of another word. *Fast* and *slow* are antonyms.

>>>> *Match the vocabulary words on the left with the antonyms on the right. Write the correct letter in the space next to the vocabulary word.*

Vocabulary Words

1. _____ **uncertain**
2. _____ **strength**
3. _____ **violent**
4. _____ **spread**
5. _____ **remote**
6. _____ **origin**

Antonyms

a. gentle
b. sure
c. enclosed
d. weakness
e. ending
f. near

COMPLETE THE STORY

>>>> Here are the ten vocabulary words for this lesson:

origin	uncertain	spread	remote	form
strength	violent	spiritual	purposes	stimulates

>>>> *There are five blank spaces in the story below. Five vocabulary words have already been used in the story. They are underlined. Use the other five words to fill in the blanks.*

Although its _____ is <u>uncertain</u>, karate in one _____ or another has <u>spread</u> across the United States.

Karate students are unsure about the _____ of their art from <u>remote</u> times. They know it <u>stimulates</u> physical, mental, and _____ growth.

After a training session, most students promise: (1) to help each other develop spiritually, mentally, and physically; (2) to listen to all instruction; (3) to meet all problems with inner <u>strength</u>; (4) to be polite to all; (5) to remember the virtue of modesty; and (6) to use karate only to stop _____ acts.

Learn More About Martial Arts

>>>> *On a separate piece of paper or in your notebook or journal, complete one or more of the activities below.*

Learning Across the Curriculum

Martial arts, including karate, have a long history in Asian countries. Research the history of karate. Write a report about what you discover.

Broadening Your Understanding

Karate is only one of several kinds of martial arts, which also include aikido, judo, tae kwan do, and jujitsu. Find out what these different kinds of martial arts have in common and how they are different. Make a grid that compares the martial arts. The rows of the grid should list the name of the martial art. The columns of the grid should list history, country of origin, and how it is used today.

Extending Your Reading

Check out one of the following books on karate from the library. Each art has a philosophy behind it. Read one of the following books. Write about the philosophy that is taught, as well as the physical moves.

Karate Basics, by Allen Queen
Karate, by Jane Mersky Leder
Facing the Double-Edged Sword: The Art of Karate, by Doyle Terren Webster
Karate Handbook, by Allen Queen

17 LIFE ON A ROPE

Mountain climbing is tough on men and women. People who climb mountains must be well trained. They are **mountaineers.** The best trained become **guides.** A good leader and great **teamwork** are needed to prevent accidents or even death.

A special hammer is made just for mountain climbing. It has a hammerhead on one end and a **pick** on the other. The hammer is used to **anchor** a piton, or large spike, into the rock **cliffs.** This piton has a hole in one end. A rope can be threaded through this hole or a **snap-ring** can be attached. The snap-ring allows the rope to slide more easily. The pick end of the hammer is used most often to chip footholds and handholds in the cliffs or in ice fields, called glaciers.

The rope used in mountain climbing is made of nylon. It is used to raise and lower mountaineers up and down the mountain. Often their lives depend on this one thin nylon rope. These people must also be able to go over or around deep holes in the ice called **crevasses.**

The weather can often be very bad high up in the mountains. Sometimes there are **blizzards.** **Snowslides,** called avalanches, may come tumbling down the mountainside. The climbers could freeze to death or be buried alive.

Even though they risk their lives on a rope, many people love this dangerous sport.

UNDERSTANDING THE STORY

>>>> *Circle the letter next to each correct statement.*

1. According to this story, in order to climb mountains a person must be
   a. at least 18 years old.
   b. able to run quickly.
   c. well trained.

2. When a sport is called dangerous, it means that
   a. there is a chance someone may be hurt or killed while doing it.
   b. it is especially difficult to do.
   c. people should not be allowed to do it.

MAKE AN ALPHABETICAL LIST

>>>> *Here are the ten vocabulary words in the lesson. Write them in alphabetical order in the spaces below.*

teamwork	mountaineers	anchor	guides	cliffs
snap-ring	snowslides	crevasses	blizzards	pick

1. _____

2. _____

3. _____

4. _____

5. _____

6. _____

7. _____

8. _____

9. _____

10. _____

WHAT DO THE WORDS MEAN?

>>>> *Following are some meanings, or definitions, for the ten vocabulary words in this lesson. Write the words next to their definitions.*

1. _____ people who climb mountains

2. _____ to fix firmly; to hold fast

3. _____ a metal ring with a clip for holding ropes

4. _____ masses of snow sliding down a mountainside; avalanches

5. _____ extreme and violent snowstorms

6. _____ working together; cooperation

7. _____ high mountain walls

8. _____ deep holes in rocks or ice

9. _____ leaders; persons who lead mountain climbers

10. _____ a pointed tool for making holes in rocks

COMPLETE THE SENTENCES

>>>> *Use the vocabulary words in this lesson to complete the following sentences. Use each word only once.*

anchor	crevasses	cliffs	mountaineers	teamwork
guides	pick	snowslides	snap-ring	blizzards

1. _____ are people who climb mountains for sport.

2. The guide warned us to watch out for _____ after it had snowed steadily for 24 hours.

3. I have the names of several _____ who can take us climbing and "show us the ropes."

4. _____ are a combination of strong winds and heavy snows.

5. One guide showed us how to _____ a large spike, or piton.

6. It took extra effort to climb the steep _____ that were covered with snow and ice.

7. No matter how strong each person is, a group needs _____ if it is going to make it to the top of a high mountain.

8. The mountaineer used a _____ to dig footholds in the cliff.

9. The _____ was greased so that the rope could slide easily.

10. You must watch out for deep holes, or _____; they are dangerous.

USE YOUR OWN WORDS

>>>> *Look at the picture. What words come into your mind other than the ten vocabulary words used in this lesson? Write them on the lines below. To help you get started, here are two good words:*

1. _____ ropes _____
2. _____ hands _____
3. _____
4. _____
5. _____
6. _____
7. _____
8. _____
9. _____
10. _____

>>>> Do you remember what a **synonym** is? It is a word that means the same or nearly the same as another word. *Sad* and *unhappy* are synonyms.

>>>> *Six of the vocabulary words for this lesson are listed below. To the right of each word are three words or phrases. Two of them are synonyms for the vocabulary word. Draw a circle around the two synonyms for each vocabulary word.*

Vocabulary Words   *Synonyms*

1. **teamwork**	cooperation	interaction	selfishness
2. **crevasses**	openings	seams	holes
3. **anchor**	lean	secure	fasten
4. **guides**	leaders	followers	teachers
5. **blizzards**	snowstorms	winter storms	warm winds
6. **cliffs**	little hills	mountainsides	rock walls

COMPLETE THE STORY

>>>> Here are the ten vocabulary words for this lesson:

teamwork	mountaineers	anchor	guides	cliffs
snap-ring	snowslides	crevasses	blizzards	pick

>>>> *There are five blank spaces in the story below. Five vocabulary words have already been used in the story. They are underlined. Use the other five words to fill in the blanks.*

An old and exciting sport is mountain climbing. <u>Mountaineers</u> should never start without training and practice. They should listen carefully to their _____. These leaders teach the climbers how to use the special tools, such as the <u>pick</u> end of the hammer. Climbers must learn how to _____ ropes to <u>cliffs</u> with a piton and a _____. They also learn how to cross or go around _____. In winter climbing, they learn the dangers of <u>snowslides</u> and _____. One of the most important lessons they learn is <u>teamwork</u>. Mountain climbing is a sport for groups, not individuals.

102

Learn More About Mountain Climbing

>>>> *On a separate piece of paper or in your notebook or journal, complete one or more of the activities below.*

Working Together

Work with a group to make a mural that explains the history of mountain climbing in North America. Draw a large map of North America. Divide up the continent. Have different people research the major mountains that have been climbed. Find out the height of each mountain, who climbed it, and when. Write this information near the place the mountain appears on the map.

Broadening Your Understanding

Describe a properly dressed mountain climber. Research all the equipment a mountain climber needs to climb a mountain safely. Write an equipment list, including the use of each piece of equipment. Or draw an illustration of a fully equipped mountain climber, with each piece of equipment identified and explained in the picture.

Learning Across the Curriculum

Mountain climbers face dangerous conditions. Research the medical problems mountain climbers most often face. Write what climbers can do to prevent these problems and what they can do if they experience them.

Did you ever wonder what a person does after being President? If you are Jimmy Carter, you work on a home. Not your home, but a home for a low-$\boxed{income}$ family.

After leaving office, Carter was $\boxed{approached}$ by Millard Fuller. Fuller asked Carter to $\boxed{lend}$ a hand to a program he had started, called Habitat for Humanity. Fuller $\boxed{founded}$ the program in 1976. The $\boxed{goal}$ of Habitat for Humanity is to build homes for low-income families. The group $\boxed{purchases}$ land and building supplies. $\boxed{Volunteers}$ donate their time to build houses. The houses are sold at $\boxed{reduced}$ prices. However, there is one catch. The buyers must give 500 hours of their own time to building new houses!

Carter $\boxed{consented}$ to help the program. He and his wife Rosalynn spend one week each year working on houses. They work alongside other less-famous volunteers. They hammer nails and saw wood. They do whatever is needed to get the job done.

The hard work of these volunteers has certainly paid off. More than 20,000 homes have been built by this program. Construction of these new homes is not limited to the United States. Habitat for Humanity homes have been built in 40 different countries. Yet, there is still more work to be done. The program plans to continue until every person has a $\boxed{decent}$ place to live.

UNDERSTANDING THE STORY

>>>> *Circle the letter next to each correct statement.*

1. Another good title for this story would be:
   a. "Presidents of the United States."
   b. "Putting a Roof over Those Without Homes."
   c. "Houses of America."

2. Though it doesn't say so, from the story you can tell that
   a. Jimmy Carter enjoys helping people.
   b. Millard Fuller hopes to become President.
   c. Jimmy Carter has found little to do since leaving the presidency.

MAKE AN ALPHABETICAL LIST

>>>> *Here are the ten vocabulary words in the lesson. Write them in alphabetical order in the spaces below.*

income	founded	approached	consented	purchases
decent	volunteers	goal	reduced	lend

1. _____   6. _____

2. _____   7. _____

3. _____   8. _____

4. _____   9. _____

5. _____   10. _____

WHAT DO THE WORDS MEAN?

>>>> *Following are some meanings, or definitions, for the ten vocabulary words in this lesson. Write the words next to their definitions.*

1. _____ agreed

2. _____ buys

3. _____ good enough; suitable

4. _____ lowered; diminished

5. _____ money received for work

6. _____ the purpose; the objective

7. _____ people who give aid and services for free

8. _____ created; set up

9. _____ to give; to provide

10. _____ reached; contacted

COMPLETE THE SENTENCES

 Use the vocabulary words in this lesson to complete the following sentences. Use each word only once.

income	reduced	purchases	volunteers	consented
approached	lend	goal	founded	decent

1. Habitat for Humanity was _____ by Millard Fuller.

2. The main _____ of the program is to provide affordable housing for all people.

3. Houses built through the program are sold to low-_____ families.

4. The construction materials are _____ by the program.

5. The homes are sold at _____ prices.

6. Many _____ donate their time to help the program.

7. Carter and his wife _____ a hand to the program.

8. They had been _____ by Millard Fuller.

9. People who buy the homes have _____ to spend 500 hours building other homes.

10. Through the program, many families now have _____ places to live.

USE YOUR OWN WORDS

Look at the picture. What words come into your mind other than the ten vocabulary words used in this lesson? Write them on the lines below. To help you get started, here are two good words:

1. _____ construction _____
2. _____ President _____
3. _____
4. _____
5. _____
6. _____
7. _____
8. _____
9. _____
10. _____

>>>> There are six vocabulary words listed below. To the right of each is either a synonym or an antonym. Remember: A **synonym** is a word that means the same or nearly the same as another word. An **antonym** is a word that means the opposite of another word.

>>>> *On the line beside each pair of words, write **S** for synonym or **A** for antonym.*

Vocabulary Words	Antonyms and Synonyms	
1. **founded**	destroyed	1. _____
2. **goal**	purpose	2. _____
3. **lend**	give	3. _____
4. **reduced**	increased	4. _____
5. **consented**	refused	5. _____
6. **decent**	suitable	6. _____

COMPLETE THE STORY

>>>> Here are the ten vocabulary words for this lesson:

decent	income	consented	purchases	reduced
founded	volunteers	approached	goal	lend

>>>> *There are five blanks in the story below. Five vocabulary words have already been used in the story. They are underlined. Use the other five words to fill in the blanks.*

   In 1976, Millard Fuller _____ Habitat for Humanity. The goal of this program is to provide _____, affordable housing for all people. Habitat for Humanity _____ land and building materials at reduced prices. _____ use the materials to build houses. The houses are sold to low-income families.

   Participation in the program is not limited to everyday citizens. Some of the volunteers are quite famous. Former President Jimmy Carter and his wife Rosalynn _____ a hand. They became involved when Fuller approached Mr. Carter. The Carters consented to help out. One week each year, the former President swings a hammer alongside other volunteers.

Learn More About Building Homes

>>>> *On a separate piece of paper or in your notebook or journal, complete one or more of the activities below.*

Learning Across the Curriculum

Imagine you have been asked to design the next house that Habitat for Humanity will build. Draw a plan that shows the layout of the house. Share your plan with the class. Explain why you decided upon the particular plan.

Broadening Your Understanding

Before starting Habitat for Humanity, Millard Fuller was a successful lawyer. Do research to find out what caused Fuller to start the program. Share your findings in an oral report to the class.

Learning Across the Curriculum

Do research to learn more about Jimmy Carter's term in office. Identify major events that occurred during the years he was President. Create a time line that highlights the accomplishments of the 39th President.

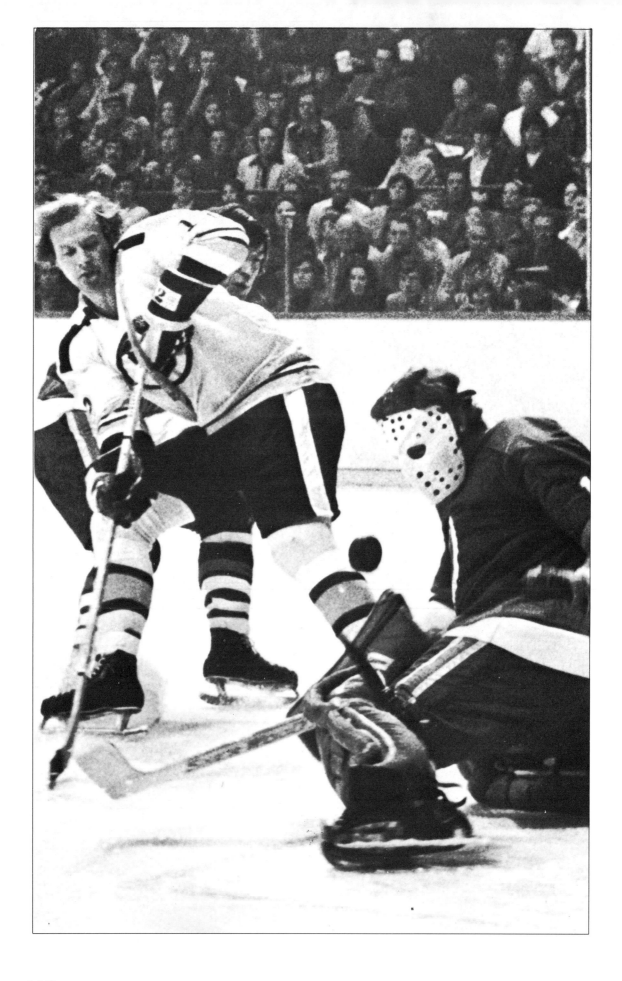

The player in the light jersey has just stolen the *puck!* He *zooms* in on the *goalie.* The other players have not gotten down the ice yet. It is player against player and goalie *versus* shooter. Will the player score for his team, or will the goalie *block* the shot?

Hockey is a *rough* sport. A player can easily be cut by a stick or knocked down on the ice. The puck is made of hard rubber. It is frozen before each game. This process makes the puck slide better on the ice. It also makes it hard as a rock. When shot at the net, the puck travels more than 100 miles an hour. In a single game, a goalie may have to block as many as 30 or 40 shots. This action takes great skill. It also takes great *courage.* Even with pads on, stopping a puck going that fast can hurt. It is no wonder that it is usually the goalie who has the most *bruises.* Some goalies even *suffer* more serious injuries.

What makes a person want to be a goalie? Most goalies will tell you that they like being where the action is. They like knowing that the whole team *depends* on them. They like doing a tough job well.

Look at that! He blocked the shot! Now he can rest a minute. Soon the players will be down at this end of the ice again, and the excitement will start all over.

UNDERSTANDING THE STORY

 Circle the letter next to each correct statement.

1. The main idea of this story is that
   a. hockey is a rough but exciting sport, especially for goalies.
   b. hockey pucks travel more than 100 miles per hour.
   c. hockey is played one-to-one rather than as a team.

2. Though this story doesn't say so, goalies probably get hurt less often these days because
   a. better pads and masks are available.
   b. hockey sticks are no longer allowed in the game.
   c. new cures for cuts and bruises have been discovered.

MAKE AN ALPHABETICAL LIST

>>>> *Here are the ten vocabulary words in the lesson. Write them in alphabetical order in the spaces below.*

rough	bruises	suffer	zooms	depends
versus	goalie	block	puck	courage

1. _____

2. _____

3. _____

4. _____

5. _____

6. _____

7. _____

8. _____

9. _____

10. _____

WHAT DO THE WORDS MEAN?

>>>> *Following are some meanings, or definitions, for the ten vocabulary words in this lesson. Write the words next to their definitions.*

1. _____ to experience something painful; to put up with

2. _____ harsh; difficult; somewhat violent

3. _____ to stop something

4. _____ a person who guards the goal in hockey

5. _____ a hard, rubber disk used in ice hockey

6. _____ marks caused by an injury that does not break the skin

7. _____ needs; relies on

8. _____ an ability to face danger or difficulty; bravery

9. _____ against

10. _____ moves quickly

COMPLETE THE SENTENCES

>>>> *Use the vocabulary words in this lesson to complete the following sentences. Use each word only once.*

rough	bruises	suffer	zooms	depends
versus	goalie	block	puck	courage

1. The goalie was able to _____ the first shot.

2. It was our goalie _____ their star player.

3. The _____ was moving very fast across the ice.

4. If you don't wear a mask when you play hockey, you may _____ a head or face injury.

5. The whole team _____ on the goalie to stop net shots.

6. Believe me, it takes a lot of _____ to stand in front of the net with sticks flying all around.

7. The _____ on the goalie's leg looked bad, but they weren't serious.

8. Do you see how that player _____ down the ice behind the puck?

9. Hockey can be a very _____ sport, so players always wear padding.

10. To be a _____, a person has to have quick reflexes and courage.

USE YOUR OWN WORDS

>>>> *Look at the picture. What words come into your mind other than the ten vocabulary words used in this lesson? Write them on the lines below. To help you get started, here are two good words:*

1. _____ ice _____
2. _____ players _____
3. _____
4. _____
5. _____
6. _____
7. _____
8. _____
9. _____
10. _____

UNSCRAMBLE THE LETTERS

>>>> *Each group of letters contains the letters in one of the vocabulary words for this lesson. Can you unscramble them? Write your answers in the lines to the right of each letter group.*

Scrambled Words	Vocabulary Words
1. clbok	_____
2. ruegcoa	_____
3. sdeepnd	_____
4. oghur	_____
5. mosoz	_____
6. sisrube	_____
7. ukpc	_____
8. lageoi	_____
9. esurvs	_____
10. feurfs	_____

COMPLETE THE STORY

>>>> Here are the ten vocabulary words for this lesson:

courage	zooms	goalie	suffer	rough
versus	block	puck	depends	bruises

>>>> *There are five blank spaces in the story below. Five vocabulary words have already been used in the story. They are underlined. Use the other five words to fill in the blanks.*

Hockey is an action-packed sport. It can also be <u>rough</u>. Often, players _____ injuries. Most of these injuries are just _____, but some are more serious. The player who probably has it the roughest is the _____. Goalies are expected to <u>block</u> shots from going into the net at all costs. The <u>puck</u> is hard and travels at a very high speed. Usually, goalies catch the puck in their huge gloves. But sometimes they must throw themselves down on the ice to block a shot. This action takes _____! Most of the time, at least one other player <u>zooms</u> down the ice to help the goalie defend the goal. At times, however, it seems to be the goalie _____ the other team. But most goalies enjoy the challenge. They like the excitement. They also like knowing that each of their teammates <u>depends</u> on them.

Learn More About Hockey

>>>> *On a separate piece of paper or in your notebook or journal, complete one or more of the activities below.*

Building Language

Look for an article from the newspaper sports section about a hockey game. Underline unfamiliar phrases in the article. Write what you think the phrase means. Check your work with another student or a dictionary.

Broadening Your Understanding

The game of hockey can be rough, and players—particularly goalies—wear equipment to protect themselves. Find out more about a goalie's equipment by interviewing a clerk at a sporting goods store. Find out what equipment is necessary, how it is made, and how it helps to protect a goalie. Write a report about what you discover.

Extending Your Reading

Wayne Gretzky is one of the most famous hockey players. Read one of the following books about him. What helped him succeed? What are some highlights of his career? Write your answers as if you were writing a paragraph in a program for a hockey game.

Gretzky, Gretzky, Gretzky!, by Meguido Zola
Wayne Gretzky, by Bert Rosenthal
Wayne Gretzky, by Thomas R. Raber

116

Ay! Torero! It is Sunday afternoon in Spain. A brave man faces a brave bull. The bull is huge, much larger than the man. Its horns are sharp. The $\boxed{matador}$ has fought many bulls before. He is well-trained and experienced. Man and bull both have $\boxed{advantages.}$ The bull's feet move quickly. It $\boxed{charges}$ the matador. The matador spins $\boxed{gracefully}$ one way. He waves his $\boxed{cape}$ another. The bull follows the cape. The watching fans cheer.

Then the matador's coworkers push sharp $\boxed{spears}$ into the bull's neck and shoulders. Its head drops low. The bull charges again. But the matador moves on his toes like a $\boxed{ballet}$ dancer. The bull misses—it does not $\boxed{gore}$ him. The horns come very close, and the crowd shouts, *"Ole!"* The bull tries again and again. The matador moves quickly out of his way each time.

The bull was $\boxed{bred}$ to be strong and brave. Its father was strong and brave. So was its father's father. It is not afraid of anything. The bull charges once more. The matador raises his sword. He thrusts it into the neck of the bull, behind its head. The bull is dead. Another day, the matador might die.

One out of every three great matadors has died a $\boxed{cruel}$ death on the horns of a brave bull.

UNDERSTANDING THE STORY

>>>> *Circle the letter next to each correct statement.*

1. Another good title for this story might be:
   a. "The Mighty Matador."
   b. "Ballet in the Sun."
   c. "A Sunday Afternoon."

2. Though it doesn't say so, from the story you can tell that large crowds of people watch the bullfights because
   a. no other sports are permitted on Sunday.
   b. the contest between matador and bull is very exciting.
   c. friends of the matadors get free passes.

MAKE AN ALPHABETICAL LIST

>>>> *Here are the ten vocabulary words in the lesson. Write them in alphabetical order in the spaces below.*

matador	bred	gracefully	charges	gore
spears	advantages	cruel	cape	ballet

1. _____
2. _____
3. _____
4. _____
5. _____

6. _____
7. _____
8. _____
9. _____
10. _____

WHAT DO THE WORDS MEAN?

>>>> *Following are some meanings, or definitions, for the ten vocabulary words in this lesson. Write the words next to their definitions.*

1. _____ a person who kills the bull in a bullfight

2. _____ things that help you; benefits

3. _____ weapons that are long poles with sharp metal points

4. _____ produced and raised with special qualities

5. _____ beautifully and smoothly

6. _____ a cloth worn over the shoulders; used in bullfighting to fool the bull

7. _____ a graceful dance

8. _____ to stab with a horn; to injure

9. _____ attacks; runs at something with speed

10. _____ not kind; brutal

COMPLETE THE SENTENCES

>>>> *Use the vocabulary words in this lesson to complete the following sentences. Use each word only once.*

cape	charges	advantages	matador	gore
gracefully	cruel	ballet	spears	bred

1. To be a _____ is the dream of many young children in Spain.

2. The matador moves as _____ as a dancer.

3. The matador looks like a _____ dancer.

4. The greatest bulls have usually been _____ to be fighters.

5. The _____ that the matador has over the bull seem few when one sees how big and strong the bull is.

6. The bull watched the movements of the matador's _____.

7. Those who are against bullfighting say it is a _____ sport.

8. The sharp horns of the bull can _____ the matador.

9. _____ are used to stab the bull and make him very angry.

10. When the bull _____ at the matador, everyone in the crowd gasps.

USE YOUR OWN WORDS

>>>> *Look at the picture. What words come into your mind other than the ten vocabulary words used in this lesson? Write them on the lines below. To help you get started, here are two good words:*

1. _____ horns _____
2. _____ danger _____
3. _____
4. _____
5. _____
6. _____
7. _____
8. _____
9. _____
10. _____

UNSCRAMBLE THE LETTERS

>>>> *Each group of letters contains the letters in one of the vocabulary words for this lesson. Can you unscramble them? Write your answers in the lines to the right of each letter group.*

Scrambled Words   **Vocabulary Words**

1. dmtraao   _____
2. grhcsea   _____
3. llbtea   _____
4. llfergacuy   _____
5. rpsaes   _____
6. tadavganse   _____
7. pcae   _____
8. erucl   _____
9. drbe   _____
10. geor   _____

COMPLETE THE STORY

>>>> Here are the ten vocabulary words for this lesson:

matador	bred	gracefully	charges	cruel
spears	advantages	gore	cape	ballet

>>>> *There are five blank spaces in the story below. Five vocabulary words have already been used in the story. They are underlined. Use the other five words to fill in the blanks.*

There you are—the <u>matador</u>. The crowd is silent. The bull looks angrily at you. Bulls are specially _____ for fighting. You have certain _____. Your friends stand with <u>spears</u> to help you. You hold a sword and a _____. But they do not seem like much against the giant animal. Now, the bull takes a few steps toward you. Then it _____. You do not move <u>gracefully</u> away. You can't even lift your feet. You do not look like a <u>ballet</u> dancer. All you can see are sharp horns ready to _____ you. You realize it could be a <u>cruel</u> death. Wake up! You're dreaming!

Learn More About Bullfighting

>>>> *On a separate piece of paper or in your notebook or journal, complete one or more of the activities below.*

Building Language

Bullfighting is popular in many Spanish-speaking countries. Words such as *toro*, *banderillero*, *picador*, *meleta*, and *estoque* are all part of bullfighting culture. Write what these words mean in both Spanish and English. Other cultures have a national sport, as well. If you are unfamiliar with bullfighting, write some words that describe a popular sport in another culture. Then write what those words mean in English.

Learning Across the Curriculum

Bullfighting is a colorful sport that has been portrayed in many forms of art. Find a work of art (pictures, books, music, and so forth) that shows or describes a bullfight. Write what you think the artist was trying to portray.

Broadening Your Understanding

Some people believe that bullfighting is a cruel sport. Others believe it is a fair contest between the bull and the matador. They find the artistry of the bullfighters thrilling. Read more about what happens during a bullfight. Decide if you think bullfighting should either be allowed or banned. Then write a letter to the editor of a newspaper in which you try to convince readers of your opinion.

A

accompany *[uh KUM puh nee]* to go along with
accomplished *[uh KAWM plished]* skilled; experienced
admiration *[ad muh RAY shun]* a feeling of wonder and approval
advanced *[ad VANSD]* moved forward
advantages *[ad VAN taij iz]* things that help you; benefits
allowed *[uh LOWD]* let; permitted
aloft *[uh LAWF]* high; above the earth
anchor *[AN kur]* to fix firmly; to hold fast
announcers *[uh NOUN serz]* people who introduce or tell about the action on TV or radio shows
appealing *[uh PEE ling]* likeable; pleasing
approached *[uh PROHCHD]* reached; contacted
aqualung *[AK wuh lung]* a dive tank that supplies air
ascending *[uh SEN ding]* going up
attention *[uh TEN shuhn]* concentration

B

ballasts *[BAL ustz]* weights used to make a gondola heavier
ballet *[bal LAY]* a graceful dance
barren *[BAIR uhn]* not producing anything; bare
benefit *[BEN uh fit]* advantage
bias *[BEYE us]* an unfair opinion or influence in favor of or against someone or something
biennial *[bye EN ee uhl]* happening every two years
bleak *[BLEEK]* dreary; swept by winds
blizzards *[BLIZ uhrdz]* extreme and violent snowstorms
block *[BLOK]* to stop something
bold *[BOHLD]* not afraid of danger; brave
booming *[BOOM ing]* with a loud, deep sound
breathe *[BREETH]* to take air in and let air out
bred *[BRED]* produced and raised with special qualities
brilliance *[BRIL yuhs]* brightness; sparkle
brilliant *[BRIL yuhnt]* spendid; magnificent
bruises *[BROO ziz]* marks caused by an injury that does not break the skin
bumble *[BUM buhl]* to act in a clumsy way

C

canals *[cuh NALZ]* waterways used like roads
canceled *[KAN seld]* stopped; done away with
cape *[CAYP]* a cloth worn over the shoulders; used in bullfighting to fool the bull
career *[kuh REER]* occupation; work
celebration *[sel uh BRAY shun]* a party in honor of something
century *[SEN chuhr ee]* a period of 100 years
characters *[KAIR ik turs]* persons in a play or movie
charges *[CHAHR jiz]* attacks; runs at something with speed

charmed *[CHAHRMD]* pleased and delighted
cliffs *[KLIFS]* high mountain walls
clumsy *[KLUM zee]* not graceful
colony *[KOL uh nee]* a settlement or town set up by a group of people
comedian *[cuh MEE dee un]* someone who tells jokes or performs in funny ways
comedy *[KOM uh dee]* something funny
competitors *[kum PET uh turz]* people who play in a contest or game
concept *[KON sept]* an idea; a plan
consented *[kuhn SENT uhd]* agreed
constantly *[KAWN stuhnt lee]* repeatedly; happening again and again
contests *[KON tests]* organized sports events
cooperate *[koh AWP uhr ayt]* to work together
coral *[KOR uhl]* a hard substance made by the skeletons of tiny sea animals
courage *[KUR ej]* an ability to face danger or difficulty; bravery
cramped *[KRAMPT]* crowded; tight
created *[kree AYT id]* invented
crevasses *[kreh VAS siz]* deep holes in rocks or ice
cruel *[KROOL]* not kind; brutal

D

decent *[DEE suhnt]* good enough; suitable
depends *[dee PENDZ]* needs; relies on
depth *[DEPTH]* the distance from top to bottom
descend *[dee SEND]* to go down
design *[di SEYEN]* forms, colors, or details arranged in a certain way
detailed *[DEE tayld]* having many small parts
developed *[dee VEL upt]* built up; grew
dim *[DIM]* only partly lighted
disappointing *[dis uh POINT ing]* not satisfying
discuss *[di SKUS]* to talk over
division *[duh VIZH uhn]* section; group
dreary *[DRIR ee]* gloomy; dull

E

economy *[ee KON uh mee]* money, goods, and services
elegantly *[EL uh gent lee]* gracefully, beautifully
energy *[EN ur jee]* enthusiasm; an inner power or ability
entranced *[en TRANST]* filled with wonder
erected *[ee REK tid]* built; constructed
eventually *[ih VEN choo wul ee]* finally, in the end
exclusively *[eks KLOO siv lee]* entirely; completely
exile *[EG zyl]* forced removal from one's homeland
experiences *[ek SPIR ee uhn ses]* all actions or events that make up a person's life
express *[eks PRES]* to make known

F

famous *[FAY muhs]* well known by many people
fans *[FANZ]* people who are enthusiastic about a performer
fashion *[FASH uhn]* current style of dress
females *[FEE maylz]* girls; women
field *[FEELD]* the type of job one does
fins *[FINZ]* rubber flippers that people wear on their feet to swim and dive
foreign *[FOR in]* coming from another country
form *[FORM]* a type; a kind
founded *[FOUN duhd]* created; set up

G

generally *[JEN uhr uhl ee]* usually; ordinarily
glow *[GLOH]* a light; to shine
goal *[GOHL]* the purpose; the objective
goalie *[GOH lee]* a person who guards the goal in hockey
gondola *[GON duh luh]* a car or basket hung under a balloon
gondolas *[GON duh luz]* long, narrow boats with a high peak at each end
gore *[GOR]* to stab with a horn; to injure
gracefully *[GRAYS fuh lee]* beautifully and smoothly
guest *[GEST]* visitor
guides *[GYDZ]* leaders; persons who lead mountain climbers
gusts *[GUSTS]* violent rushes; sudden outbursts

H

habit *[HAB it]* an outfit worn by a nun
helicopter *[HEL i kawp tuhr]* aircraft with circular blades
helium *[HEE lee um]* gas used to fill balloons
hired *[HYRD]* given a job
honest *[ON est]* truthful; not phony
host *[HOHST]* the main announcer on a show; someone giving a party for invited guests
hush *[HUSH]* quiet, sudden silence

I

imaginary *[i MAJ i ner ee]* existing only in the mind or imagination; unreal
improvise *[IM pruh veyez]* to make up
included *[in KLOO uhd]* made part of; involved
income *[IN kuhm]* money received for work
inflated *[in FLAYT id]* filled up
inhabitants *[in HAB uh tunts]* persons or animals who live in a place
interested *[IN trist id]* wanting to know more about something; concerned
ironic *[eye RON ik]* something that is opposite to what you would expect
islands *[EYE lands]* bodies of land surrounded by water

J

javelin *[JAV lin]* a spear used in sports events

K

key *[KEE]* most important; central

L

lend *[LEND]* to give; to provide

M

matador *[MAH tuh dor]* a person who kills the bull in a bullfight
mountaineers *[moun tuh NEERZ]* people who climb mountains
mouthpiece *[MOUTH pees]* a part of the scuba equipment that the diver holds in the mouth
movement *[MOOV ment]* crusade; organized effort
mumble *[MUM buhl]* to speak in an unclear way with the lips not open enough

N

national *[NASH uh nuhl]* having to do with a whole country
nature *[NAT chuhr]* the natural world
nervous *[NUR vus]* uneasy, uncomfortable
neurosurgery *[noor oh SUR jur ee]* operations on the brain, spinal cord, or nerves

O

observers *[uhb ZERV uhrs]* viewers
obstacles *[OB stih kulz]* barriers; difficulties
obtain *[uhb TAYN]* to gain possession of
origin *[OR uh jin]* the beginning; where something comes from

P

passengers *[PAS un jurz]* people who travel in a bus, boat, train, or plane
penal *[PEE nul]* involving punishment
pick *[PIK]* a pointed tool for making holes in rocks
pleasure *[PLEZH uhr]* delight; enjoyment
poverty *[PAWV uhr tee]* state of being poor
precious *[PRESH us]* having great value
prefer *[pree FUR]* to want one thing instead of another
preparation *[prep uh RAY shuhn]* readiness
previously *[PRE vee us lee]* earlier; before
pride *[PREYED]* good feelings about yourself; self-respect
professional *[proh FESH uhn uhl]* having to do with earning a living in a job that requires certain skills
provide *[pruh VEYED]* to give; to supply
puck *[PUK]* a hard, rubber disk used in ice hockey
purchases *[PER chuh sez]* buys
purposes *[PUR puh siz]* goals; aims

Q

qualify *[KWAHL uh feye]* to prove oneself worthy
quotas *[KWOH tuhs]* shares; positions held for a certain group

R

racism [RAYS iz uhm] a belief that one's own race is superior to another
rare [RAIR] scarce; only a few left
rarely [RAIR lee] not often; seldom
rate [rayt] measured quantity
reduced [ri DOOSD] lowered; diminished
regulated [REG yuh layt id] kept in working order; controlled
remote [ree MOHT] far off in time
respected [rih SPEKT id] admired
ridiculous [ri DIK yuh luhs] funny, silly
risks [RISKS] hazards; possibilities of danger
roam [ROHM] to move about as one pleases; wander
rough [RUF] harsh; difficult; somewhat violent
rupture [RUP chuhr] to break open; to burst

S

scheduled [SKE joold] happening at definite times
schools [SKOOLZ] large numbers of fish swimming together
screen [SKREEN] a surface or area on which movies or television images are shown
scuba [SKOO buh] gear that allows breathing underwater: <u>s</u>elf-<u>c</u>ontained <u>u</u>nderwater <u>b</u>reathing <u>a</u>pparatus
senior [SEEN yur] older; more than age 55
severe [suh VEER] very harsh or difficult; stern
shadows [SHAD ohz] areas of darkness or shade
sketch [SKECH] an incomplete drawing
skills [SKILZ] abilities that come from practice
smothered [SMUTH uhrd] to cut off oxygen supply; suffocated
snap-ring [SNAP ring] a metal ring with a clip for holding ropes
snowslides [SNOH slydz] masses of snow sliding down a mountainside; avalanches
sought [SAWT] searched for; tried to find
spears [SPIRS] weapons that are long poles with sharp metal points
species [SPEE sheez] animals that have some common characteristics or qualities
spiritual [SPIR ih choo uhl] holy or religious; having to do with the soul

spread [SPRED] gone all over
stimulates [STIM yuh layts] excites; makes more active
strength [STRENTH] power; force
stride [STREYED] a step or style of walking
style [STEYEL] a way of doing things
suffer [SUF uhr] to experience something painful; to put up with
surfacing [SUR fuh sing] coming to the top of the water
survival [sur VEYE vul] staying alive; existing
system [SIS tuhm] a plan; a set of rules

T

tasks [TASKS] jobs; assignments
teamwork [TEEM wurk] working together; cooperation
threat [THRET] something dangerous that might happen
tickets [TIK uhts] notices you get from a police officer for breaking the law

U

ultimately [UHL tuh mit lee] finally; at last
uncertain [un SUR tuhn] not known for sure; doubtful

V

various [VER ee uhs] different kinds; more than one
versus [VUR suhs] against
violent [VEYE uh lunt] wild; roughly forceful
visitors [VIZ it uhrz] people who visit; sightseers
volunteers [vawl uhn TERZ] people who give aid and services for free

W

water-bus [WA tur bus] a canal boat with a motor that carries many passengers

Y

youngster [yung stuhr] child

Z

zooms [ZOOMZ] moves quickly